my revision notes

AQA A2
LAW
CRIMINAL LAW UNITS 3A AND 4A
AND CONCEPTS OF LAW UNIT 4C

Sally Russell

HODDER
EDUCATION

The Publishers would like to thank the following for permission to reproduce copyright material:

Acknowledgements

AQA material is reproduced by permission of AQA.

Hachette UK's policy is to use papers that are natural, renewable and recyclable products and made from wood grown in sustainable forests. The logging and manufacturing processes are expected to conform to the environmental regulations of the country of origin.

Orders: please contact Bookpoint Ltd, 130 Park Drive, Abingdon, Oxon OX14 4SE. Telephone: +44 (0)1235 827720. Fax: +44 (0)1235 400454. Lines are open 9.00a.m.–5.00p.m., Monday to Saturday, with a 24-hour message answering service. Visit our website at www.hoddereducation.co.uk.

© Sally Russell 2014

First published in 2014 by
Hodder Education,
An Hachette UK Company
338 Euston Road
London NW1 3BH

Impression number   10 9 8 7 6 5 4 3 2 1
Year   2018 2017 2016 2015 2014

Cover photo © iStock/Thinkstock
Artwork by Datapage (India) Pvt. Ltd.

Typeset in Cronos Pro-Light 12/14 by Datapage (India) Pvt. Ltd.
Printed in Spain

A catalogue record for this title is available from the British Library.

ISBN 978 14718 07121

Get the most from this book

Everyone has to decide his or her own revision strategy, but it is essential to review your work, learn it and test your understanding. These Revision Notes will help you to do that in a planned way, topic by topic. Use this book as the cornerstone of your revision and don't hesitate to write in it — personalise your notes and check your progress by ticking off each section as you revise.

☑ **Tick to track your progress**

Use the revision planner on page 4 to plan your revision, topic by topic. Tick each box when you have:

● revised and understood a topic
● tested yourself
● practised the exam questions and gone online to check your answers and complete the quick quizzes.

You can also keep track of your revision by ticking off each topic heading in the book. You may find it helpful to add your own notes as you work through each topic.

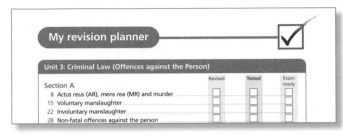

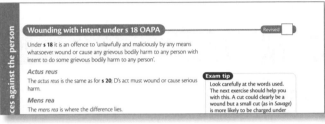

Features to help you succeed

Exam tips and summaries

Throughout the book there are tips to help you boost your final grade. Summaries provide advice on how to approach each topic in the exams, and suggest other things you might want to mention to gain those valuable extra marks.

Typical mistakes

Examples of typical mistakes candidates make and how you can avoid them.

Exam practice

Practice exam questions are provided for each topic. Use them to consolidate your revision and practise your exam skills.

Now test yourself

These short, knowledge-based questions provide the first step in testing your learning. Answers are at the back of the book.

Striving for an A/A*?

These activities will help you to understand each topic in an interactive way.

Online

Go online to check your answers to the exam questions and try out the extra quick quizzes at **www.therevisionbutton.co.uk/myrevisionnotes**.

Check your understanding

Use the questions that have been set at the end of the topic to make sure that you understand each topic. Answers are at the back of the book.

Points for an essay

Important points you should be aware of and be prepared to discuss fully in an essay.

Examples and case examples

Examples are provided throughout the book to illustrate the application of the law to different scenarios; and case examples examine real cases.

My revision planner

Unit 3: Criminal Law (Offences against the Person)

Unit 4: Criminal Law (Offences against the Property)

Unit 4: Concepts of Law

Countdown to my exams

6–8 weeks to go

- Start by looking at the specification — make sure you know exactly what material you need to revise and the style of the examination. Use the revision planner on page 4 to familiarise yourself with the topics.
- Organise your notes, making sure you have covered everything on the specification. The revision planner will help you to group your notes into topics.
- Work out a realistic revision plan that will allow you time for relaxation. Set aside days and times for all the subjects that you need to study, and stick to your timetable.
- Set yourself sensible targets. Break your revision down into focused sessions of around 40 minutes, divided by breaks. These Revision Notes organise the basic facts into short, memorable sections to make revising easier.

Revised ☐

4–6 weeks to go

- Read through the relevant sections of this book and refer to the exam tips, exam summaries and typical mistakes. Tick off the topics as you feel confident about them. Highlight those topics you find difficult and look at them again in detail.
- Test your understanding of each topic by working through the 'Now test yourself' questions in the book. Look up the answers at the back of the book.
- Make a note of any problem areas as you revise, and ask your teacher to go over these in class.
- Look at past papers. They are one of the best ways to revise and practise your exam skills. Write or prepare planned answers to the exam practice questions provided in this book. Check your answers online and try out the extra quick quizzes at **www.therevisionbutton.co.uk/ myrevisionnotes**.
- Use the revision activities to try different revision methods. For example, you can make notes using mind maps, spider diagrams or flash cards.
- Track your progress using the revision planner and give yourself a reward when you have achieved your target.

Revised ☐

One week to go

- Try to fit in at least one more timed practice of an entire past paper and seek feedback from your teacher, comparing your work closely with the mark scheme.
- Check the revision planner to make sure you haven't missed out any topics. Brush up on any areas of difficulty by talking them over with a friend or getting help from your teacher.
- Attend any revision classes put on by your teacher. Remember, he or she is an expert at preparing people for examinations.

Revised ☐

The day before the examination

- Flick through these Revision Notes for useful reminders, for example the exam tips, exam summaries and typical mistakes.
- Check the time and place of your examination.
- Make sure you have everything you need — extra pens and pencils, tissues, a watch, bottled water, sweets.
- Allow some time to relax and have an early night to ensure you are fresh and alert for the examinations.

Revised ☐

My exams

A2 Criminal Law LAW03

Date: ....

Time: ....

Location:...

A2 Criminal Law LAW04

Date: ....

Time: ....

Location:...

Unit 3 Section A: Criminal Law (Offences against the Person)

Introduction

This unit is divided into five chapters covering:

- murder
- voluntary manslaughter
- involuntary manslaughter
- non-fatal offences against the person
- defences.

Most offences are made up of *actus reus* and *mens rea*. This unit continues from AS on these elements so you should have a good base to build on. However, you need more depth at this level so will need to develop what you know. The scenarios are more complex and you will need to consider possible defences and be able to evaluate the different areas of law (except involuntary manslaughter).

Murder, voluntary manslaughter and involuntary manslaughter could come together in one scenario. Non-fatal offences against the person are also usually seen together. The defences may come into any question, as may issues of *actus reus* and *mens rea*, such as causation and proving intent.

The examination

- Examinations take place once a year in June. (The last January exams were in 2013.)
- The exam lasts 1 hour 30 minutes.
- You can choose one scenario from two on the law you have studied for this unit.
- Two questions will be asking you to apply the relevant law to the scenario given.
- The third question will be an essay question asking you to evaluate an area of law within the unit.
- Essay questions may cover any area from the unit except involuntary manslaughter. For defences you will only be asked to evaluate two of these so revise two defences thoroughly.
- You must answer all three questions on the scenario you choose.
- Each question is worth 25 marks.
- All three questions carry 10 marks for AO1 and 15 marks for AO2.
- One question will carry an additional 5 marks for quality of written communication (AO3).

Help from the exam board

- The AQA website has a lot of important and useful information and guidance. It tells you what you need to cover in each topic and explains the Assessment Objectives (AO1, AO2 and AO3).
- There are plenty of past examination papers, together with mark schemes and examiners' reports.
- It is important to look at these for revision because they give you helpful guidance on what should be covered in order to reach the higher grades.

Preparing for the exam

- You need to be prepared to answer questions on all the topics in the unit. The material in this Revision Guide will help you do this, but you should also look at previous papers, mark schemes and reports to prepare properly for the exam.
- To gain high marks, answers need to be relevant to the question asked. It is important to be selective and not just to write down all you know about an area. This approach does not gain marks because it indicates that you do not know how to apply the *relevant* law.
- The level of detail needed will depend on how many areas of law are covered. Where there are several areas to be covered, less detail will be expected.
- You should revise the material thoroughly, so that you go into the exam with confidence.
- You need to understand the law, not just to be able to reproduce it. You will need to adapt it to answer questions that are slightly different from those that you may have answered before.
- You should practise answering questions under exam conditions so you can learn to manage your time efficiently.

Use of authorities

- You will need to refer to authorities in support of your answer; these include examples, cases and Acts of Parliament.
- For cases, the date of the case is not important and with long or complicated case names it is sufficient to use a shortened version. Examiners will know which case you mean. Criminal cases are usually written *R v*, but in most law textbooks (including this Revision Guide) the cases are referred to by the name of the defendant only.
- For Acts of Parliament, it is important to include the date and to know the different section numbers for the different parts of the *actus reus* and *mens rea*.

1 *Actus reus* (AR), *mens rea* (MR) and murder

Introduction

This chapter includes the three key areas for murder:

- *actus reus*
- *mens rea*
- the law specific to murder.

Actus reus

Revised ☐

Actus reus can include:

- conduct
- circumstances
- consequences.

Here is a quick recap:

Actus reus				
Conduct		**Circumstances**	**Consequences**	
Act	**Omission**		**Causation**	
Must be voluntary.	Only if a duty arises.		Factual	Legal
Except state of affairs crimes, e.g. *Winzar (1983)*.	If there is a duty to act, failing to act can result in liability, e.g. *Miller (1983)*.	Seen in the actual definition of a crime, e.g. murder must be of a 'human being'.	Apply the 'but for' test – *White (1910)*.	D made a significant contribution – *Cheshire (1991)*. Any intervening act was foreseeable – *Roberts (1971)*. Does the 'thin skull' rule apply? – *Blaue (1975)*.

Conduct: Acts and omissions

- *Actus reus* must be voluntary.
- Except in state of affairs crimes (e.g. *Winzar* – being drunk on the highway).
- *Actus reus* must coincide with *mens rea* but an act can be treated as continuing – *Fagan (1986)*.
- Or as a series of acts – *Thabo Meli (1954)*.
- *Actus reus* can be by an omission.
- Only if there is a duty to act.

Key cases on duty to act

Type of duty	Case example	Brief explanation
A duty undertaken voluntarily	*Stone and Dobinson (1977)*	Her brother and his partner had undertaken a voluntary assumption of responsibility to care for his sister so were liable for manslaughter for failing to do so.
A contractual duty	*Pittwood (1902)*	He had a contractual duty to close the railway crossing so was liable for manslaughter when he failed to do so and someone was killed by a train.
A duty because of a relationship	*Gibbins and Proctor (1918)*	Parents have a duty to take care of their child so can be liable for murder if they intentionally withhold food. G had a duty of relationship as a parent. P had a duty undertaken voluntarily as in *Stone and Dobinson* above.
A duty to put right a dangerous situation D has created	*Miller (1983)*	He accidentally started the fire but then had a duty to do something about it, so was liable for arson for failing to act.

Causation

● If the *actus reus* includes a consequence, causation will be important.

● These are called 'result' crimes. Murder is an example as there must be death as a consequence of D's act or omission. ABH is another example; here harm must result.

● So D's act or omission must cause the result (death) in fact and in law.

Key cases on causation

Factual causation The 'but for' test	'But for' D's act or omission the result would not have occurred (*White 1910*).
Legal causation The *de minimis* rule – D's act need not be the sole cause but must be more than trifling or minimal.	Poor medical treatment will not usually break the chain if D's action made a 'significant' contribution to the death (*Cheshire 1991*).
	Turning off life support will not break the chain (*Malcherek 1981*).
The chain of causation – D will be liable for the full consequences if the chain of causation is not broken.	A foreseeable intervening act will not break the chain (*Roberts*) but a daft one might (*Williams 1992*).
The 'thin skull' rule.	A particular weakness in V will not break the chain (*Blaue*).

Now test yourself

Tested

1 What three 'C's are part of the *actus reus*?
2 When can an omission amount to *actus reus*?
3 Why was Miller liable for what appears to be an accident?
4 How would you apply the rule on factual causation to the facts in *Pagett (1983)*?
5 How would you apply the rules on legal causation to *Pagett*?
6 State whether the following break the chain of causation and note any exception:
   a) a refusal of hospital treatment
   b) poor hospital treatment
   c) where the resulting harm or death is caused by V running away from an attack.

Answers on page 116

Mens rea

- There are three types of *mens rea*:
  - intention (direct or indirect)
  - subjective recklessness
  - gross negligence.
- *Mens rea* can be transferred from one victim to another – *Latimer (1886)*.
- *Mens rea* must coincide with *actus reus* but there may be a continuing act (*Fagan*) or a series of acts (*Thabo Meli*).

Key cases on *mens rea*

Mens rea	Brief explanation	Case
Direct intent	It is D's decision to bring about the result (the result is D's aim or purpose).	*Mohan (1976)*
Indirect intent	The result is a virtual certainty and D appreciates this.	*Nedrick (1986)/Woollin (1998)*
Subjective recklessness	D recognises the risk of the result but goes ahead anyway.	*Cunningham (1957)* Also *Gemmell and Richards (2003)*, where the HL confirmed that all recklessness is now subjective.
Gross negligence	D is criminally negligent – for manslaughter only.	*Adomako (1994)*
Transferred malice	D intends to hit X but hits Y instead – the intent is transferred from X to Y.	*Latimer (1886)*
Coincidence of AR and MR	The AR may be continuing so it coincides with a later MR.	*Fagan (1986)*

Murder

- The classic seventeenth-century definition of murder has evolved through case law but there is no statutory definition.
- Essentially murder is the unlawful killing (AR conduct) of a human being (AR circumstance) with malice aforethought (MR intent) which results in death (AR consequence).

Actus reus for murder

- The killing of a human being.
- Murder is a result crime.
- D's conduct must cause the death in fact and in law (see 'Causation' on the previous page).

Human being

- A foetus is not a human being for the purpose of a murder conviction.
- If the foetus is injured and dies from that injury after being born, that may be murder.
- *A-G's Reference (No 3 of 1994) 1997.*

An omission to act may be murder

Murder can be by omission as well as a positive act if a duty is owed to the victim. In *Gibbins and Proctor*, the Ds lived together with the man's daughter. They failed to give her food and she died. The CA upheld their murder convictions. If food is withheld with intent to cause grievous bodily harm then it would be murder. This brings us on to *mens rea*.

Mens rea for murder

- The unlawful killing must be done with 'malice aforethought'.
- This has been interpreted as meaning with intention.
- The *mens rea* for murder is an intention to kill or cause grievous bodily harm – *Vickers (1957)*.
- Confirmed by the HL in *DPP v Smith (1960)*.
- Intention may be direct – it is D's decision to cause death or serious injury – *Mohan*.
- Intention may be indirect – there is a virtual certainty that death or serious injury will result and D appreciates this – *Nedrick/Woollin* (see opposite under *Mens rea*).

Case example

In *Stringer* (2008), a boy had been accused of murder and arson after a fire started at the bottom of the stairs in his house. Several of his family were sleeping upstairs at the time and his brother died in the fire. There was evidence that he had started the fire, although he denied this. The boy was only fourteen with a low IQ. He argued that he did not have the required intent for murder. The CA referred to *Woollin* and held that the distinction between the two parts of the test should be made clear to the jury. However, if this test was applied to the facts of the case there was clear evidence for the jury to find intent. There could only be one answer to the first part because it is a virtual certainty that death or serious injury can result from a fire. Also, even with his age and low IQ he must have realised this, so the second part of the test would also be satisfied.

Exam tip

If something is obvious discuss it very briefly, e.g. you could say that there is clear intent to kill so no question of *mens rea* and so move quickly on to the other issues such as causation. Alternatively, you could say that the issue of causation is clear but it may be difficult to prove intent and so discuss *mens rea* and the *Nedrick* test in more detail.

Typical mistake

It is common for students to spend too long on irrelevant issues. You need to be selective. A problem question on murder may well include issues on *actus reus*, *mens rea* or the partial defences (as well as general ones) but very rarely all of these. If the matter is obvious, say so briefly and move on.

Now test yourself

Tested ☐

7 What is the first part of the *Woollin* test?
8 How would it be applied to the facts in *Stringer*?
9 What is the second part of the *Woollin* test?
10 How would this be applied to the facts in *Stringer*?
11 Note the principle of the following cases:

Case	Principle
Fagan (1986)	
Stone and Dobinson (1977)	
Roberts (1971)	
Cheshire (1991)	
Blaue (1975)	
DPP v Smith (1960)	

Answers on page 116

Summary

Actus reus

✔ The unlawful killing of a human being.

✔ D's act or omission caused the death both factually (*White*) and legally (*Cheshire*).

Mens rea

✔ Intent to kill or seriously injure – *Vickers/Smith*.

✔ It is D's decision to bring about the result – *Mohan*

OR

✔ Death or serious injury is a virtual certainty and D appreciates this – *Nedrick/Woollin*.

✔ *Mens rea* can be transferred from the intended victim to the actual victim – *Latimer*.

✔ *Mens rea* and *actus reus* must coincide but can be a series of acts – *Thabo Meli*.

Exam tip

In problem questions you need to take a logical approach. Read the facts carefully and then state and apply the law, using relevant cases in support in order to reach a sustainable conclusion. Only the most recent cases are needed for explaining the law, although older ones can be used if the facts are particularly relevant. For essay questions, you will need the older law so you can explain any problems and possible improvements. The table below will help with this.

Key cases and statute law on the development of the law on intent and the difficulties caused by the different words used in relation to foresight

Case	Development	Type of foresight: natural, probable, possible or certain?
Vickers (1957)/DPP v Smith (1960)	HL held that the *mens rea* for murder is intention to kill or cause grievous bodily harm/ serious injury.	Foresight of death or serious injury as a natural and probable result.
Criminal Justice Act (1967)	Made the test subjective – what D foresaw not what the reasonable person would foresee.	D intended or foresaw a result of his actions as being a natural and probable consequence.
Moloney (1985)	HL held that foresight of the result was not proof of intent only *evidence* of intent.	D foresaw death or serious injury as a probable certainty or natural consequence.
Hancock and Shankland (1986)	*Moloney* guidelines were followed but HL held that 'natural consequence' was misleading and preferred 'probable'.	The greater the probability, the more likely it was foreseen and thus intended.
Nedrick (1986)	CA formulated a new test which would provide evidence from which the jury can 'infer' intent.	Death or serious injury was a virtual certainty as a result of D's actions. D appreciated that such was the case.
Walker and Hayles (1990)	CA applied *Nedrick* but confused the issue again by referring to *Hancock* and probability.	Foresight of death or serious injury as a very high degree of probability would be enough.
Woollin (1998)	HL confirmed *Nedrick* test for jury to 'find' intent but not clear whether this would be proof or evidence.	Death or serious injury was a virtual certainty as a result of D's actions. D appreciated that such was the case.
Matthews and Alleyne (2003)	CA applied *Nedrick* test but held that evidence of intent is not proof of intent.	As above.

Check your understanding: 1 Application practice

1 What Is a result crime and what is the significance in terms of *actus reus*?

2 Read the facts of *Pagett* and then use your knowledge of the *actus reus* and *mens rea* of murder to apply the law to these facts (you can refer to questions 4 and 5 in the 'Now test yourself' box on page 9).

Answers on page 116

Points for an essay

- D is not usually liable for an omission but can be in certain circumstances. There is a degree of uncertainty in such cases, e.g. *Bland (1993)*, *Gibbins and Proctor*.
- The rules on what will break the chain of causation may be difficult for a jury to understand.
- The thin skull rule seems unfair.
- The law on intent has developed but is arguably still unclear.
- Murder is a common law offence. Should there be a statutory definition?
- The *mens rea* for murder is intent to kill or seriously injure. For such a serious crime should it only be intent to kill?
- Having a mandatory life sentence for murder means the judge cannot take circumstances into account when sentencing, e.g. in euthanasia cases.

Reforms

The Law Commission recommended a three-tier structure for homicide which could address some of these problems:

- first-degree murder (killing with intent to kill or with intent to cause serious harm knowing the conduct carried a risk of death)
- second-degree murder (killing with intent to cause serious harm or where there is a defence of provocation (now loss of control) or diminished responsibility as now for voluntary manslaughter), and
- manslaughter (killing without intent, as now for involuntary manslaughter, but with *mens rea* needed for some kind of harm).

Only the first of these would have a mandatory life sentence. These recommendations have not been taken up by the government.

Check your understanding: 2 Essay practice

3 Can you give an argument against having a mandatory life sentence for murder?

4 Would the Law Commission's recommendations change the approach to sentencing in a case where D intended to cause serious harm but not to kill?

5 Would the Law Commission's recommendations change the approach to sentencing in euthanasia cases?

Answers on page 116

Summary

- ✔ *Actus reus* and *mens rea* are needed before someone is guilty of murder.
- ✔ An omission can be enough for the *actus reus* if there is a duty to act.
- ✔ Murder is a result crime so make sure you can apply the rules on factual and legal causation to establish *actus reus* (see questions 4 and 5 in the 'Now test yourself' box on page 9).
- ✔ *Mens rea* is direct or indirect intent. Be sure you understand the ruling in *Nedrick* and can apply it to given facts (see questions 8 and 10 in the 'Now test yourself' box on page 11).
- ✔ There is no statutory definition of murder, so know your cases well, especially where a principle has been established (as in *Nedrick*, opposite).

- ✔ The general law on *actus reus* and *mens rea* prepares you for answering a murder 'problem' question:
  - Murder can be committed by an omission (*Gibbins and Proctor*).
  - Murder is a result crime so it must be proved that D's act caused death factually (*White*) and in law (*Cheshire*).
  - The *mens rea* of murder is intent which can be direct (*Mohan*) or indirect (*Nedrick/Woollin*).
- ✔ For an essay, you need to concentrate on understanding the problems in the law so that you can produce a critique, along with a discussion of any reforms (see 'Points for an essay' and 'Check your understanding: 2 Essay practice' above).

Exam practice

Usually essay questions cover both murder and the partial defences (voluntary manslaughter) so the exam question is in the next chapter. Look back at this chapter before attempting it.

Striving for an A/A*?

Go to the Law Commission website and look at the 'A–Z of projects'. Find 'Murder, manslaughter and infanticide' (the 2006 report). The project documents will be found at the side of a short commentary by the Commission. Quotations and discussions from this will greatly enhance an essay.

2 Voluntary manslaughter

Introduction

This chapter covers loss of control and diminished responsibility.

- Both of these are partial defences to a charge of murder.
- They **only** apply to a murder charge.
- If successful, the conviction is for manslaughter not murder.
- This allows the judge discretion when sentencing.

Loss of control   Revised ☐

Loss of control replaces the previous defence of provocation. The law is now found in **s 54** and **s 55** of the Coroners and Justice Act 2009, which came into force in October 2010.

S 54 states:

> '(1) Where a person ("D") kills or is a party to the killing of another ("V"), D is not to be convicted of murder if:
>
> (a) D's acts and omissions in doing or being a party to the killing resulted from D's loss of self-control,
>
> (b) the loss of self-control had a qualifying trigger, and
>
> (c) a person of D's sex and age, with a normal degree of tolerance and self-restraint and in the circumstances of D, might have reacted in the same or in a similar way to D.'

Loss of self-control s 54

- The killing must have been caused by the loss of self-control; this is a new requirement under the 2009 Act.
- There must be loss of control, not just self-restraint. In *Cocker (1989)*, D had finally given way to his wife's entreaties to ease her pain and end her life. His defence failed as the evidence showed he had not lost control. This would still apply for the new law.
- Under **s 54 (2)** there is no longer a need for the loss of control to be sudden. This is new.
- In *Thornton (1992)*, she waited in the kitchen till her husband was asleep before she killed him. This would no longer matter regarding the time lapse, but could indicate she did not lose control at all. By the time she killed him she had calmed down. Similarly in *Ahluwalia (1992)*.
- **S 54 (4)** states that the defence is not allowed if D acted in a 'considered desire for revenge'.
- Note the words 'resulted from D's loss of self-control'; it must have caused the killing.

The qualifying triggers s 55

The loss of control must be triggered by:

'D's fear of serious violence from V against D or another identified person; or

a thing or things done or said (or both) which –

(a) constituted circumstances of an extremely grave character, and

(b) caused D to have a justifiable sense of being seriously wronged.

Or a combination of both of these.'

- The violence need not be directed at D. In *Pearson (1992)*, a boy killed his father because of violence directed at his brother; this is still the law.

- The 'things done or said' must be 'extremely grave' and 'justifiably' cause D to feel 'seriously' wronged. This is stricter than the old law.

- In *Doughty (1986)*, the crying of a baby was said to amount to what was then called provocation. The new defence would be unlikely to succeed. The crying of a baby is not *extremely grave* nor is a jury likely to believe that it caused D to have a *justifiable* sense of being *seriously* wronged.

Excluded triggers

- Under **s 55 (6)**, if the thing 'done or said' constituted sexual infidelity, it is to be disregarded.

- Under the old law, it would have been allowed.

- Also excluded under **s 55 (6)** are situations where D has incited either the fear of violence or the thing done or said, in order to have the excuse to use violence.

Now test yourself

Tested

1 To what charge does the Coroners and Justice Act 2009 apply?
2 What three things need to be proved for **s 54**?
3 What amounts to a qualifying trigger?
4 What 'trigger' is excluded by the Act?
5 What does the Act say about revenge?

Answers on pages 116–17

Would a normal person of D's sex and age have reacted in the same way?

- This is similar to the law as stated in *Holley (2005)*, but made a little clearer by the Act.

- In *Holley*, D was an alcoholic and, while drunk, he killed his girlfriend with an axe after finding out she had slept with another man. She also taunted him about his lack of courage.

- The Privy Council said that D was to be judged against the standard of a person having 'ordinary powers of self-control', not against the standard expected of a particular D in the same position.

- Alcoholism is therefore no longer a 'relevant matter' for the jury when deciding whether a reasonable person would have done what D did.
- D's age and sex are relevant, as before.
- The standard of control expected is that of a person of the same age and sex with normal levels of tolerance and self-restraint.
- This is an objective test.
- Even if the jury accepts that a normal person might have lost control, if they believe such a person would not have reacted in the same way the defence will fail.

Case example

In *Asmelash* (2013), D had been drinking with another man and they got into a fight and D killed him. He said the deceased had made him so angry that he lost control. The judge said the jury should consider whether a person of D's sex and age with a normal degree of tolerance and self-restraint and in the same circumstances, but unaffected by alcohol, would have reacted in the same or a similar way. The CA agreed with the judge that the consumption of alcohol should be ignored.

In D's circumstances

S 54 (3) states that 'the circumstances of D' is a reference to all of D's circumstances other than those whose only relevance to D's conduct is that they bear on D's general capacity for tolerance or self-restraint.

- So several factors can be taken into account, such as a history of abuse (*Thornton/Ahluwalia*), depression, etc.
- Although sexual infidelity is excluded as a trigger it can be taken into account as a circumstance.
- This was decided by the CA in *Clinton* (2012).
- Circumstances whose only relevance to D's conduct is that they bear on a general capacity for tolerance or self-restraint are excluded – **s 54 (3)**.
- So things that made D lose control more easily, such as being drunk or aggressive by nature, are excluded.

Check your understanding: 1 Application practice

1 In *Ibrams and Gregory* (1981), the Ds and a girl had been terrorised by V. They planned to entice V to the girl's bed and then the Ds would attack him. They carried out the planned attack several days later, and killed V. At their appeal against a conviction for murder, the CA held that the defence failed because there was no sudden loss of control; the attack was planned and carried out over several days. Explain how the new law applies to these facts.

Answers on page 117

Exam tip

The law is still fairly complex but try to learn the basic definitions so you can apply them accurately to a scenario. For essay questions you are likely to need to discuss the old law as well as the reforms so make sure you know some of the older cases too, especially if they were controversial or contradictory.

Diminished responsibility

Diminished responsibility comes under the Homicide Act 1957 **s 2 (1)**, as amended by **s 52** of the Coroners and Justice Act 2009. This section came into force in October 2010 and states:

'A person who kills or is a party to the killing of another is not to be convicted of murder if he was suffering from an abnormality of mental functioning which:

(a) arose from a recognised medical condition,

(b) substantially impaired D's ability to:

understand the nature of his conduct; or

form a rational judgement; or

exercise self-control

and

(c) provides an explanation for D's acts and omissions in doing or being a party to the killing.'

Abnormality of mental functioning

● In *Byrne (1960)*, an abnormality of mind (the old expression) was said to be 'a state of mind so different from that of ordinary human beings that the reasonable man would term it abnormal'.

● This is likely to remain the same for abnormality of mental functioning.

Abnormality of mental functioning and intoxication

● An abnormality caused by taking drugs or drink will not suffice (confirmed in *Dowds* below).

● Alcoholism, now usually referred to as Alcohol Dependency Syndrome (ADS), will suffice as it is a medical condition.

● In *Dietschmann (2003)*, D savagely attacked someone while suffering depression. He was also drunk. The HL held that the abnormality did not have to be the only cause of the killing but that D had to show that even without the drink he had sufficient 'abnormality of mind' (now mental functioning) to impair his responsibility.

● So being drunk will not suffice but if there is another cause of the abnormality (such as depression) the jury must ignore the drink and concentrate on that.

● In *Wood (2008)*, D had been diagnosed with ADS and killed in a frenzied attack while drunk. The CA said the jury should consider whether D's responsibility was substantially impaired because of the syndrome and ignore any drink taken voluntarily.

● In *Dowds (2012)* (after the 2009 Act came into force), D argued that acute intoxication was a recognised medical condition. He and his partner had a long history of drunkenness and violence, and both had been drinking when he attacked and killed her. The CA held that the new law did not change the rule that voluntary intoxication was not capable of establishing the defence of diminished responsibility.

A recognised medical condition

- Medical evidence will be needed but many disorders seen in cases before the Act will still be relevant.
- In *Wood*, the disorder was Alcohol Dependency Syndrome.
- In *Martin (2001)*, a Norfolk farmer was convicted of murder after killing an intruder. His defence was based on diminished responsibility due to a 'paranoid personality disorder'.
- In *Thornton* and *Ahluwalia* it was 'battered woman syndrome'.

Substantially impaired D's ability

- In *Lloyd (1967)*, the court said the impairment need not be total but must be more than trivial or minimal.
- This is likely to remain the same under the new law.
- Unlike the old law under **s 2**, as amended by the Coroners and Justice Act, it is not the mental responsibility that must be substantially impaired, but the ability to do one of three things:
  - to understand the nature of his/her conduct, or
  - to form a rational judgement, or
  - to exercise self-control.
- For example, in *Byrne*, the new defence could succeed because his ability to exercise self-control was impaired.

Provides an explanation for D's acts and omissions

- There must now be some causal connection between D's abnormality of mental functioning and his/her conduct.
- The abnormality must cause the killing or make a significant contribution to it.

> **Exam tip**
>
> Cases such as *Thornton* and *Ahluwalia* show the overlap between loss of control and diminished responsibility, so be prepared to discuss both defences in cases where factors such as 'battered woman syndrome' are apparent. Long-term abuse is a characteristic to attribute to the 'normal person' for loss of control, but over a long period it could lead to an abnormality of mental functioning caused by a recognised medical condition.

Now test yourself

Tested ☐

From which cases did the following principles come?

6 That sexual infidelity may be relevant to the circumstances of D, even though excluded by **s 55**.

7 That an 'abnormality of mind' (now mental functioning) for diminished responsibility is one that reasonable people would term abnormal.

8 An abnormality caused by alcoholism may be accepted as diminished responsibility.

9 Impairment of responsibility need not be total but must be more than trivial.

10 Where there is evidence of intoxication as well as another cause of 'abnormality', the jury should ignore the intoxication.

Answers on page 117

> **Case example**
>
> In *Zebedee (2011)*, D killed his father who was suffering from Alzheimer's disease and was incontinent. He said that he snapped after remembering alleged abuse by his father he suffered as a child. He argued both diminished responsibility and loss of control. For the first he said his ability to exercise control had been impaired by an adjustment order resulting from the earlier abuse. As for loss of control, he said this was caused by his father whistling a tune over and over, soiling himself and making a gesture which recalled the abuse. The jury rejected both defences.

> **Exam tip**
>
> As with loss of control, the law is still fairly complex but try to learn the basic definitions so you can apply them accurately to a scenario. For essay questions you are likely to need to discuss the old law as well as the reforms so make sure you know some of the older cases too, especially if they were controversial or contradictory.

Check your understanding: 2 Application practice

In *Freaney (2011)*, a woman had killed her severely autistic eleven-year-old son. Mrs Freaney denied murder but admitted manslaughter on the grounds of diminished responsibility. Her son needed 24-hour care and help with dressing, washing, brushing his teeth and eating. He was not toilet trained and still wore nappies. She murdered her son using her coat belt and when she was sure he was dead she lay down on the bed beside him and tried to commit suicide. The jury decided she was suffering under extreme mental stress at the time she strangled her son. Her plea of diminished responsibility was accepted and in July 2011 she was sentenced to a supervision order.

2 What was Mrs Freaney charged with and what did she plead in defence?

3 What is the effect of a successful defence and why is that important for D?

4 Under the Coroners and Justice Act 2009 **s 52** what must be proved for this defence?

5 What three things might be impaired?

6 How would you apply the new law to this case?

Answers on page 117

Key cases on voluntary manslaughter

Case	Brief facts	Principle
Thornton (1992)	D killed her husband while he slept on the sofa after going to the kitchen to calm down.	The loss of control defence could still fail as D did not appear to lose control.
Clinton (2012)	D killed his wife after she had told him she was having an affair and he had seen graphic images of her and her lover on Facebook.	Sexual infidelity is not a qualifying trigger but can be taken into account when considering D's circumstances.
Byrne (1960)	A man was unable to control his sexual desires and strangled a woman.	An abnormality is something ordinary people would deem abnormal.
Lloyd (1967)	Case needed for principle only.	The impairment need not be total but must be more than trivial.
Dietschmann (2003)	D savagely attacked someone while suffering depression and he was also drunk.	The abnormality did not have to be the only cause of the killing but the jury should ignore any intoxication.
Wood (2008)	D had been diagnosed with ADS and killed in a frenzied attack while drunk.	Confirms that the jury should ignore any drink taken voluntarily.
Dowds (2012)	D had been drinking when he attacked and killed his girlfriend.	The new law does not change the rule that voluntary intoxication is not capable of establishing diminished responsibility.

Summary

For loss of control under **s 54** of the Coroners and Justice Act 2009:

✔ D must have lost self-control.

✔ D's loss of self-control must have caused the killing.

✔ The loss of self-control must be triggered by something specified in **s 55**.

✔ A normal person of D's sex and age would have reacted in the same way in D's circumstances.

Under **s 55 (1)** the loss of control must be triggered by:

✔ D's fear of serious violence from V against D or another identified person; or

✔ a thing or things done or said (or both) which:
  ● constituted circumstances of an extremely grave character, and
  ● caused D to have a justifiable sense of being seriously wronged.

✔ Excluded by the Act are **s 54 (4)** revenge and **s 55 (6)** sexual infidelity (see *Clinton*).

For diminished responsibility under **s 2** of the Homicide Act as amended by the Coroners and Justice Act 2009:

✔ There must be an abnormality of mental functioning

✔ which arises from a 'recognised medical condition'

✔ and substantially impaired D's ability to do one or more of three specified things

✔ and provides an explanation for D's acts and omissions.

✔ The specified things are:
  ● to understand the nature of his/her conduct, or
  ● to form a rational judgement, or
  ● to exercise self-control.

Points for an essay

- Loss of control has been clarified by the Coroners and Justice Act 2009; older cases on what characteristics could be taken into account (e.g. *Smith*) showed the law was in a mess.
- The removal of the need for the loss of control to be sudden seems fair.
- The triggers include fear of serious violence so could cover abused women cases.
- Cases such as *Thornton* and *Ahluwalia* may still fail, however, because of the need for a loss of control.
- The Law Commission had suggested removing any need for loss of self-control but this was rejected.
- In other ways the new law is stricter than the old law, especially as regards the triggers.
- Sexual infidelity is excluded as a trigger but is often what leads someone to lose control.
- The defence is not allowed if D acted in a 'considered desire for revenge'.
- Diminished responsibility is not a satisfactory alternative for abused women as it indicates they are mentally unbalanced.
- The requirement of a 'recognised medical condition' is clearer than the old law and will allow for more modern syndromes to be taken into account.
- However, 'abnormality of mental functioning' is still difficult for the jury to understand and medical evidence is often complex.
- Where there is evidence of intoxication as well as another cause of 'abnormality', the jury has to perform an almost impossible task of separating the one from the other (*Dietschmann*).
- There is an overlap between diminished responsibility and loss of control where the killing is due to a mental state such as depression or long-term abuse (*Ahluwalia* and *Thornton*).
- The difficulties of these defences for the jury could lead to inconsistency.
- The burden of proof is on D for diminished responsibility.
- If the mandatory life sentence for murder were abolished these defences would not be necessary.

Check your understanding: 3 Essay practice

7 Pick three of the above points and develop them to produce a paragraph which you could use in an essay on the improvements and/or remaining problems with these defences.

Answers on page 117

Exam practice

AQA January 2012

Despite some recent reforms, there are still criticisms to be made of the current law on murder and voluntary manslaughter. Consider relevant criticisms of that law, and suggest any reforms that may be appropriate.

Hint: Before attempting this question look back at the problems in relation to murder as the question covers both areas.

[25 marks]

Answers online

Online

Striving for an A/A*?

Go to the Law Commission's website and look at the 'A–Z of projects'. Find 'Partial defences to murder' (the 2004 report). Quotations and discussions from this will enhance an essay and help you to see how far the Coroners and Justice Act took up the Law Commission's suggestions.

3 Involuntary manslaughter

Introduction

There is no evaluation of this area so you only need the current legal principles and a few case examples to support your application of the law. There is also therefore no essay question practice in this chapter, but there is some extra application practice.

There are two types of involuntary manslaughter:

● gross negligence manslaughter
● unlawful act manslaughter.

Gross negligence manslaughter Revised ☐

The rules on gross negligence manslaughter were clarified by the HL in *Adomako (1994)*.

An anaesthetist had failed to monitor a patient during an operation. The patient later died as a result. The doctor was accused of manslaughter. The CA held that in order to prove gross negligence manslaughter there must be:

● a risk of death
● a duty of care
● breach of that duty
● gross negligence as regards that breach, which must be sufficient to justify criminal liability.

Risk of death

In *Misra (2004)*, the CA confirmed the *Adomako* requirements and said that a risk of death was needed, not just a risk of harm.

Duty of care

● The duty is the same as in the civil law.
● In *Wacker (2002)*, the judge referred to the 'ordinary principles of the law of negligence'.
● In *Stone and Dobinson* (see Chapter 1 page 9), they had no *mens rea* for murder but were guilty of gross negligence manslaughter. They had a duty to his sister as they had voluntarily taken her into their care.

Now test yourself Tested ☐

What type of duty was owed in the following cases seen in Chapter 1 (pages 8–14)?

1 *Stone and Dobinson*
2 *Pittwood*
3 *Gibbins and Proctor*

Answers on pages 117–18

Breach of duty and gross negligence

- Breach occurs where D fails to reach the standard of care expected.
- It ties in with risk of death and gross negligence.
- In *Stone and Dobinson*, they were expected to do more to take care of the sister so had breached their duty.
- The jury must then consider whether, having regard to the risk of death, D was sufficiently (grossly) negligent to justify criminal liability.

Exam tip

It is sometimes difficult to be sure of the result when it is a decision for the jury, but you should try to apply the law to the facts to reach an arguable conclusion. It is acceptable to put forward a case for and against D being found guilty.

Typical mistake

Students often avoid reaching a conclusion because it is a matter for the jury. You should do the best you can to fit the law to the facts.

Check your understanding: 1 Application practice

1 In *Wood and Hodgson (2003)*, a ten-year-old girl was visiting the Ds. She found some ecstasy tablets hidden in a cigarette packet and took some. There was evidence that they had hidden the tablets, and that they had attempted to treat her, but they did not call an ambulance for some time. She later died in hospital. They were charged with gross negligence manslaughter. Apply the rules to the facts of this case to decide if they were guilty.

Answers on page 118

Unlawful act manslaughter

Revised

This type of manslaughter is also called constructive manslaughter. It is 'constructed' from three elements:

- an unlawful act
- which is dangerous, and
- which causes death.

An unlawful act

- The act must be a crime – *Lamb (1967)*.
- It must be an act, not an omission.
- In *Khan and Khan (1998)*, suppliers of drugs did not get help for a person who had overdosed on heroin and the court said that this did not amount to unlawful act manslaughter as there was no 'act', only an omission (to get help).

Now test yourself

Tested

Look up the following cases seen in Chapter 1 (pages 8–14). There was no *mens rea* for murder so it was manslaughter rather than murder in each.

4 In *Nedrick* what was the unlawful act?
5 In *Woollin* what was the unlawful act?
6 In *Pagett* what was the unlawful act?

Answers on page 118

Which is dangerous

- This is an objective test – *Church (1967)*.
- The question is whether a reasonable person would see a risk of some harm resulting from the act.
- The risk must be of 'some harm' not just fear – see *Dawson* below.

Case example

Compare these two cases.

In *Dawson (1985)*, during an attempted robbery of a garage, Ds had frightened the victim with an imitation pistol. He suffered from a heart condition and subsequently died. They were found not guilty of manslaughter because a reasonable person would not have been aware of the heart condition, and so would not see the act as dangerous. The court recognised that fear could be foreseen, but as physical harm could not be, the act was not dangerous in the true sense.

In *Watson (1989)*, burglars entered a house and saw an elderly man, but continued with their act of burglary. He died of a heart attack. The man's frailty was obvious and so a reasonable person would see the danger of the act.

Exam tip

Take care when applying the rules in a problem scenario. In *Dawson*, the question was whether the act was dangerous. The answer was 'no' because a reasonable person would not know of the heart condition. If the act *had* been dangerous then D would 'take the victim as he finds him'. Thus, D would be liable for the death even though a person without a heart condition would not have died.

Typical mistake

Students often misunderstand the point of *Dawson* and confuse it with the thin skull rule. This rule may well be relevant but it will only apply *after* the act is found to be unlawful and dangerous. It is a causation issue.

Now test yourself   Tested

Look up these cases and then answer the questions.

- In *Cato (1976)*, D supplied, and assisted V to take, heroin which resulted in death.
- In *Dalby (1982)*, D had supplied drugs and then V injected himself.
- In *Kennedy (1999)*, D mixed the drug and handed the syringe to V who injected himself.

7 Were Cato and Dalby found guilty or not guilty?
8 What is the essential difference between the cases of *Cato* and *Dalby*?
9 Which case do you think the defence would have relied on in *Kennedy*?
10 Which case do you think the prosecution would have relied on?
11 Was Kennedy found guilty at his trial?
12 What happened in the House of Lords following a retrial and another appeal in 2007?
13 Which case did the House of Lords' decision follow?

Answers on page 118

Which causes death

Causation is an important element in manslaughter, as it is in murder. The rules are the same:

- D's act or omission must cause death factually:
  - 'But for' D's actions the victim would not have died.
- D's act or omission must cause death legally:
  - D made a significant contribution to the death.
  - Nothing broke the chain of causation between D's action or omission and the death.

This last has caused some conflicting case law.

Look at *Cato*, *Dalby* and *Kennedy* in the previous exercise. It now seems clear that:

- If the victim self-administers the drug, the supplier will not be liable for manslaughter if V dies, because this breaks the chain of causation.
- There must be an active participation in order for D to be liable.

Check your understanding: 2 Application practice

Using the same three cases as the 'Now test yourself' box on page 23, apply the law on unlawful act manslaughter as regards the 'dangerous' and 'causes death' aspects to:

2 *Nedrick*

3 *Woollin*

4 *Pagett*

Answers on page 118

Mens rea
Revised

- There is no special *mens rea* for this type of manslaughter.
- It is the *mens rea* for the unlawful act.
- Which is either intent or subjective recklessness, most often the latter.
- There is, therefore, no need to prove *mens rea* as regards the death, only the unlawful act.

Key cases on involuntary manslaughter

Case	Brief explanation	Legal principle
Adomako (1994)	An anaesthetist had failed to monitor a patient during an operation.	Set out the tests for gross negligence manslaughter.
Misra (2004)	Also a medical case (failing to identify an infection in a patient).	Confirmed *Adomako* and that there must be a risk of death, not just harm.
Wacker (2002)	D brought illegal immigrants into the UK and many died due to poor ventilation.	A duty is established on the 'ordinary principles of the law of negligence'.
Lamb (1967)	D killed a friend while playing with a gun; no unlawful act.	For constructive manslaughter the act must be unlawful.
Church (1967)	D thought the woman he knocked out was dead and threw her in the river to get rid of the body.	Although he saw no risk of harm a reasonable person would see this as a dangerous act.
Dawson (1985)	Ds held up a garage and the man died of a heart attack.	A reasonable person would not see this as dangerous as there was no evidence of a heart problem.
Watson (1989)	Ds burgled a house and an old man died of a heart attack.	*Dawson* was distinguished as here it was obvious V was old and frail so a reasonable person would see this as dangerous.
Khan and Khan (1998)	Ds failed to get help to someone in a coma to whom they had supplied drugs.	No duty of care for gross negligence manslaughter. Cannot commit unlawful act manslaughter by omission.
Kennedy (1999)	D supplied drugs and V died after self-injecting.	An adult self-injecting breaks the chain of causation.

You may find you are unsure what the *mens rea* is, e.g. the unlawful act is often criminal damage (including arson) and you may not have covered this area. If you are not sure just say D must have either intent or recklessness to cause criminal damage and that will cover it, as long as you then apply this to the facts. The next 'Check your understanding' (3 Application practice) will help with this.

Typical mistake

Students often say that D must have intent or subjective recklessness to cause a death but this is not the case. There is no need to prove *mens rea* as regards the death, only the unlawful act itself.

Exam tip

Both types of manslaughter

If the question asks you to discuss D's liability for manslaughter only discuss involuntary manslaughter. A discussion of murder (or voluntary manslaughter, which is only used for a murder charge) will gain no marks at all. However, be prepared to discuss both types. For example, if there is doubt as to whether a duty is owed, you could state the rules for gross negligence manslaughter, explain there may be a problem proving a duty and go on to unlawful act manslaughter as an alternative. If there is an omission to act, you can use *Khan* to support the fact that unlawful act manslaughter won't apply and then go on to apply the rules on gross negligence manslaughter.

Check your understanding: 3 Application practice

Again using the same three cases explain the *mens rea* in:

5 *Nedrick*

6 *Woollin*

7 *Pagett*

Answers on page 118

Summary

For gross negligence manslaughter there must be:

✔ a risk of death – *Adomako/Misra*

✔ a duty of care – *Stone and Dobinson/Wacker*

✔ breach of that duty – *Stone and Dobinson*

✔ gross negligence – *Adomako/Misra*.

For unlawful act manslaughter there must be:

✔ an unlawful act – *Lamb*

✔ which is dangerous – *Church*

✔ which causes death – *Kennedy*

✔ the act must be a crime – *Lamb*

✔ it must be an act, not an omission – *Khan and Khan*

✔ whether it is dangerous is defined by whether a reasonable person would see a risk of some harm resulting from the unlawful act – *Church*

✔ the risk must be of 'some harm', not just fear – *Dawson*

✔ the *mens rea* is for the unlawful act.

That's all three types of homicide, so here's a quick recap:

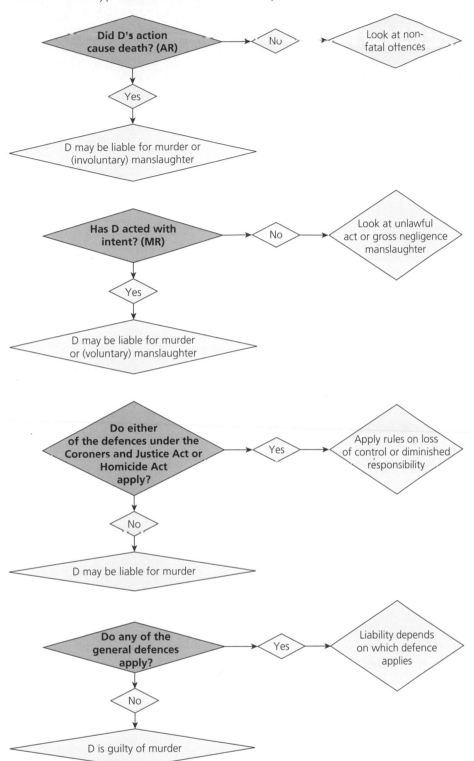

Did D's action cause death? (AR)
- No → Look at non-fatal offences
- Yes → D may be liable for murder or (involuntary) manslaughter

Has D acted with intent? (MR)
- No → Look at unlawful act or gross negligence manslaughter
- Yes → D may be liable for murder or (voluntary) manslaughter

Do either of the defences under the Coroners and Justice Act or Homicide Act apply?
- Yes → Apply rules on loss of control or diminished responsibility
- No → D may be liable for murder

Do any of the general defences apply?
- Yes → Liability depends on which defence applies
- No → D is guilty of murder

Exam practice

There is no essay question on this area; you do not have to evaluate it. The 'Check your understanding' examination practice should have prepared you for a problem question.

4 Non-fatal offences against the person

Introduction

There are five non-fatal offences which you need to revise. Be sure to note the differences between them so that you can recognise the appropriate offence in an examination scenario:

- assault
- battery
- assault occasioning actual bodily harm
- grievous bodily harm
- wounding with intent.

Assault and battery   Revised ☐

- These are two separate offences, together called 'common assault'.
- The definitions for assault and battery come from the common law (hence the name).
- The Criminal Justice Act 1988 **s 39** classifies them as summary offences so they are charged under this section.
- They often go together, but the law for each is different.

Assault

- The *actus reus* of assault is to cause someone to apprehend immediate and unlawful personal violence.
- The law has developed through cases but this definition was confirmed in *Ireland (1997)*.
- Assault can include words, or even silence:
  - In *Ireland*, Lord Steyn said '*The proposition that a gesture may amount to an assault, but that words can never suffice, is unrealistic and indefensible.*'
  - In *Constanza (1997)* (a case of stalking), and *Ireland* (silent telephone calls), there was an assault.
- Words may prevent an assault by indicating it will not occur – *Turbeville v Savage (1669)*.
- It is the effect on the victim which is important:
  - If the other person is not afraid there can be no assault – *Lamb*.
  - The fear must be of immediate force but this is quite wide.

Apprehend immediate violence or force

- In *Smith v Chief Superintendent of Woking Police Station (1983)*, a 'peeping Tom' looked through the victim's bedroom window at night. She apprehended (feared) immediate and unlawful personal violence even though the man was outside.

Exam practice answers and quick quizzes at **www.therevisionbutton.co.uk/myrevisionnotes**

- In *Ireland*, the victim was held to have apprehended immediate violence through silent telephone calls, and in *Constanza* through stalking.
- These cases show that the term 'immediate' is widely interpreted.
- They also show that there does not have to be a physical threat; words or even silence will be enough.

Mens rea

The *mens rea* for assault matches the *actus reus*. It is:

- intention to cause the victim to apprehend unlawful and immediate violence, or
- recklessness as to whether the victim apprehends unlawful and immediate violence.

Battery

- The *actus reus* of battery is the application of unlawful force to another.
- Assault and battery often, but not always, go together.

> **Example**
>
> Sam shouts abuse at Tim and then punches him. This would be both assault (shouting abuse) and battery (the punch). If Sam only threatened Tim by shouting abuse it would be assault alone. If Tim did not see the punch coming, e.g. Sam was behind him, he would not be afraid so this would only be battery.

- The force can be slight, as in *Thomas*, where touching clothes was said to amount to a battery.
- Battery can be a continuing act. In *Fagan*, the battery was applying unlawful force by driving on to the police officer's foot; leaving the car there meant the unlawful force continued up until the time he had *mens rea*.
- Battery can be indirect. In *DPP v K (1990)*, a schoolboy put acid in a hot air drier and another pupil was injured. The court held such an indirect act could be a battery.
- Another example is *Haystead (2000)*, where a man punched a woman who then dropped her baby. This was held to be a battery on the baby.
- Battery cannot be committed by omission (stated in *Fagan*).

Now test yourself

1. What amounted to assault in:
   a) *Constanza*?
   b) *Ireland*?
2. What was said to be unlawful force in *Thomas*?
3. Look up the facts of *Fagan*.
   a) What was the battery?
   b) What principle developed in regard to *actus reus* in this case?
   c) Was it treated as an act or an omission?

Answers on page 118

Unlawful force

In *Collins v Wilcock (1984)*, a police officer who took hold of the woman's arm was acting unlawfully so this amounted to a battery. However, some force may be lawful.

- If the victim consents to the force this will make it lawful.
- Consent can be implied in some situations:
  - in sports such as rugby where using force is part of the game
  - in surgical procedures, or a trip to the dentist.
- Acting in self-defence also makes force lawful.
- Both consent and self-defence are covered in Chapter 5 (pages 36–50).

Mens rea

As with assault, the *mens rea* is intent or subjective recklessness.

- For battery it is intent or recklessness as to whether unlawful force is applied.
- D must intend or see the risk of unlawful force being applied to another.

Assault occasioning actual bodily harm (ABH) under s 47 Offences Against the Person Act 1861 (OAPA)

Revised

S 47 provides that a person convicted of 'any assault occasioning actual bodily harm shall be liable to imprisonment for not more than five years'.

This means that for **s 47** you need an assault (which covers assault and battery, remember) plus actual bodily harm.

Actus reus

- There must first be an assault or battery.
- The harm must be more than trivial – *Chan Fook (1997)*.
- Harm includes psychiatric harm but not 'mere emotions such as fear, distress or panic' – *Chan Fook*.
- In *DPP v Smith (Michael) (2006)*, cutting off someone's hair was sufficient harm as it was held to be part of the body.
- Finally, the assault or battery must 'occasion' the harm – an issue of causation.

Mens rea

- *Mens rea* is intention or subjective recklessness.
- It is only *mens rea* for the assault or battery that is needed.
- D need not intend or be reckless as to any harm.
- This was confirmed by the HL in *Savage (1991)*.

Exam tip

The definition of ABH has been the subject of much case law so it is important to know the cases well. Remember you only need to prove *mens rea* for the assault or battery, not for any harm. You will also need to decide which type of harm comes within each of these offences so that you choose the appropriate one and apply the correct law. If you think the harm is too serious for **s 47** you may need to go on to **s 18** or **s 20**. These are dealt with on the following pages.

Typical mistake

Too often students apply the law to the facts to establish *actus reus* but then say that D must intend or be reckless as to causing harm. This is not the case; if D intends or is reckless as to causing fear or applying force this is enough.

Case example

In *Savage*, a girl threw some beer at another girl and the glass slipped, cutting the victim. The throwing of the beer was a battery (applying unlawful force) and she intended to throw it so had *mens rea*, too. She argued she neither intended nor saw the risk of harm, but was found guilty of ABH. She had the *actus reus* and *mens rea* for battery, plus some harm had been caused and this was enough.

Check your understanding: 1 Application practice

1 In *Roberts*, a man grabbed at a girl's coat while in a car and she jumped out and was injured. Apply the law you have revised so far in this chapter to these facts to decide if he was guilty, and if so of which offence.

Answers on page 118

Points for an essay on problems with ABH

- It seems unfair that a person can be convicted of ABH when only having *mens rea* for an assault or battery.
- Assault under **s 47** means both assault and battery, which is confusing.
- Neither assault nor battery is defined in any statute.
- The word 'occasioning' is obscure and the word 'actual' seems unnecessary.
- Actual bodily harm seems to extend to a huge range of harm.
- It now includes psychiatric harm (*Chan Fook/Ireland*) which is perhaps an advance.

Grievous bodily harm (GBH) under s 20 OAPA

Revised

Under **s 20** it is an offence to 'unlawfully and maliciously wound or inflict any grievous bodily harm upon any other person, either with or without any weapon or instrument'.

So there are two parts to the offence:

- wounding, or
- inflicting grievous bodily harm.

Actus reus

- A wound requires a break in the continuity of the skin – *Eisenhower (1983)*.
- Grievous bodily harm means really serious harm (*Smith 1961*) but serious harm is enough (*Saunders 1985*).
- In *Burstow*, a campaign of harassment which led to V suffering severe depressive illness was charged under **s 20**. The HL held serious psychiatric harm could be GBH.
- In the joint appeals of *Burstow and Ireland (1977)* (see ABH opposite), the HL held that there was no difference between 'cause' (**s 18**) and 'inflict' (**s 20**).
- In *Bollom (2004)*, a baby suffered bruising to several parts of the body. The court held that although bruising would normally be ABH at most, it could amount to GBH in the case of a young child.

Mens rea

- The word 'maliciously' in **s 20** has been interpreted as meaning with intent or subjective recklessness – as for most crimes.
- The main importance as regards *mens rea* is that there is no need to intend or see the risk of serious harm.
- Only *mens rea* for some harm is required.
- This was confirmed in *Mowatt*.

Exam tip

The *Bollom* case shows that the effect on the victim may affect the charge. This case could be used to support a charge of GBH instead of ABH if the situation involved someone elderly or vulnerable. This might be useful if you are unsure of which charge is most appropriate.

Wounding with intent under s 18 OAPA

Under **s 18** it is an offence to 'unlawfully and maliciously by any means whatsoever wound or cause any grievous bodily harm to any person with intent to do some grievous bodily harm to any person'.

Actus reus

The *actus reus* is the same as for **s 20**; D's act must wound or cause serious harm.

Mens rea

The *mens rea* is where the difference lies.

- **S 20** says 'with intent to do some grievous bodily harm'.
- Intention is needed, recklessness is not enough.
- D must intend 'to do some grievous bodily harm', i.e. D must intend **serious** harm – *Saunders*.
- Intent applies as for murder (*Nedrick/Woollin*); see Chapter 1 (pages 10–13).
- One final difference with the *mens rea* for **s 18** is that it includes intent to resist arrest, and in this case there is no need to intend serious harm.
- Recklessness is enough – as long as there was intent to resist arrest.

> **Exam tip**
>
> Look carefully at the words used. The next exercise should help you with this. A cut could clearly be a wound but a small cut (as in *Savage*) is more likely to be charged under **s 47**. Words such as fracture, internal bleeding, stitches, prolonged hospital treatment, etc. should point you at **s 20** or **s 18**. Mention of a weapon points towards **s 18**, as, if someone has a weapon they probably intend serious harm. Also remember a young or vulnerable victim may push the charge up (*Bollom*).

Now test yourself

4 Which offence(s) do you think the following types of harm would come under? Give a reason for your answer and/or support it with a case.
- a bruise
- several bruises
- a fractured skull
- a small cut
- a large gash
- a broken bone
- a grazed knee
- internal injuries

5 Note down the following facts and principles and add the case name. Keep this for final revision of the key cases.

Brief facts	Principle	Case
Stalking a woman caused fear of force.	Silence may be enough for an assault.	
Case needed for principle only.	If D has *mens rea* for some harm that will be enough for **s 20**; there is no need to have MR for serious harm.	
Case needed for principle only.	Grievous means serious harm.	
Silent telephone calls to woman caused fear.	Words or even silence may be enough for an assault.	
A boy put acid in a dryer and another boy was injured.	A battery can be indirect.	
A woman threw a glass of beer at another woman.	For ABH there is no need to foresee the risk of harm – only of an assault (or battery).	
D placed his hand on the hilt of his sword and said 'If it were not assize time I would not take such language from you'.	Words may prevent an assault by indicating it will not occur.	
A man locked in a room got in a panic and was injured trying to get out.	Mere emotions such as fear, distress or panic are not enough for actual bodily harm; nor is trivial harm.	
A man grabbed a girl's coat and she was injured when she jumped from the car.	A foreseeable act by the victim will not break the chain of causation.	
A boy was hit in the eye by a pellet.	Wound means an open cut.	

Answers on pages 118–19

Points for an essay on problems with s 20 and s 18

- As with **s 47**, the language is obscure and words like 'maliciously' and 'grievous' probably meant something different when the Act was passed.
- Wound is any breaking of the skin, which could be a small cut.
- The *actus reus* is for **serious** harm but the *mens rea* is for **some** harm.
- As with **s 47**, it is unfair that the charge can be higher than whatever D had *mens rea* for.
- The maximum sentence for **s 20** is five years, which is the same as for **s 47**, a lesser offence.
- The maximum sentence for **s 18** is life, which is a huge difference when the *actus reus* is the same.

Points for an essay on reforms

In 1993, the Commission produced a report (**No 218**) and draft Bill on the non-fatal offences against the person. This never received parliamentary time but in 1998 the government produced its own Bill incorporating most of the recommended changes. A new project is due in 2014 (see 'Check your understanding' box on page 34).

Name of proposed offence	Explanation of proposed offence	Current offence
Intentional serious injury	Clause 1: intentionally causing serious injury.	**S 18**
Reckless serious injury	Clause 2: recklessly causing serious injury.	**S 20**
Intentional or reckless injury	Clause 3: intentionally or recklessly causing injury.	**S 47**
Assault	Clause 4: intentionally or recklessly applying force to or causing an impact on the body of another; or intentionally or recklessly causing another to believe force is imminent.	Common assault (assault and battery)

This would be much clearer than the current law.

- The offences are redefined and in all of them the *mens rea* matches the *actus reus*.
- In each case the word 'cause' is used.
- Injury is defined to include both physical and psychiatric harm.
- The Bill has not yet received parliamentary time, which is a problem in itself.

Exam tip

Essay questions

When evaluating the law be sure to include a discussion of proposed reforms and not just a critique of the law. This will show not only that you understand the problems, but also that you can see how the reforms may help to solve some of them.

Check your understanding: 2 Application practice

Look at the following brief scenarios. Decide on the most appropriate offence and apply the law you have revised in this chapter to the facts, using cases in support.

2 Sergio grabbed at Sandy's jacket and as she tried to get away she fell over, grazing her knee.
3 Tracey threw a book at Sam who jumped aside and pushed over an elderly woman, who cried out in pain.
4 The elderly woman had brittle bones and broke her leg when she fell.
5 Andy leant out of the train window as it pulled out of the station and shouted at Viktor, saying he will beat him next time he sees him.
6 Steffi pulled out a knife and slashed Lena's cheek.

Answers on page 119

Check your understanding: 3 Essay practice

Go to the Law Commission website, find offences against the person under 'A–Z of projects' and answer the questions below. These refer to a new project being set up to reconsider the law on this area in 2014 so will be useful when discussing the problems of the law as it currently stands, and the proposed reforms.

7 What problem is widely recognised by the Law Commission?

8 What does the LC say is a problem with the structure of the Act?

9 What problem regarding sentencing is highlighted?

10 What does the LC say about the *actus reus* for **s 18** and **s 20**?

11 What are the main aims of the new project?

12 Do you think these reforms will help, if they are implemented?

Answers on pages 119–20

Answers on pages 119–20

Exam tip

'Problem' questions

For 'problem' questions it is important that you show you understand the law and how it applies by keeping things relevant and referring as often as possible to the facts given. Examiners frequently complain about how many students ignore this advice, which is given in most examiners' reports.

Example

The scenario says 'Jim attacked Mark with a knife and when in hospital having several stitches removed …'.

It is not enough to say Jim can be charged with **s 18** and then just regurgitate all the law you know on that offence. Better to say Jim will be charged under **s 18** because he 'attacked Mark with a knife' and so this indicates that he intended to cause serious harm. It also says Mark had 'several stitches' so refer to this and say it means there was a wound as both layers of the skin would have been broken (*Eisenhower*). Then go on to deal with other issues as relevant, possibly also dealing with **s 20** if you feel it may be hard to prove on the facts that Jim intended to cause serious harm.

Typical mistake

Students too often don't pick up on the words the examiner uses and pick the wrong offence (see 'Now test yourself' question 4 on page 32 for guidance on this). Another common mistake is to 'write all you know' and cover all the offences when clearly some are inappropriate. Make an effort to pick out the offence which is indicated and then go on to an alternative only if there is any doubt. For example, you may chose **s 18** and find that it is hard to prove intent to cause serious harm, so you would go on to **s 20**.

Summary

Assault – to cause the victim to apprehend immediate and unlawful personal violence.

Battery – the unlawful application of force to another.

✔ *Mens rea* is intent or subjective recklessness to carry out the *actus reus*.

S 47 assault occasioning actual bodily harm

(ABH) – an assault or battery which results in harm.

✔ Harm may be fairly minor and includes psychiatric harm but not trivial harm – *Chan Fook*.

✔ *Mens rea* is intent or subjective recklessness to carry out the *actus reus* of an assault or battery.

✔ There is no need to have *mens rea* as regards any harm – *Savage*.

✔ ABH is a result crime so causation is important.

✔ If the victim acts reasonably and foreseeably this will not break the chain of causation – *Roberts*.

S 20 grievous bodily harm or malicious wounding

(GBH) – inflicting serious harm or a wound.

✔ Wound means an open cut – *Eisenhower*.

✔ Grievous means serious – *Saunders*.

✔ *Mens rea* is intent or subjective recklessness to inflict some harm – *Mowatt*.

S 18 wounding with intent – causing serious harm or a wound.

✔ *Mens rea* is intent (only) to cause grievous bodily harm – *Parmenter (1991)*.

There are several different 'assaults' and lots to remember, so here is a guide to working through a problem question.

- Identify the offence or offences.
- Define them and explain the AR/MR as you work through the facts given.
- Only discuss relevant offences; don't try to cover them all.
- Note that for **s 47** and **s 20** the *mens rea* doesn't match the *actus reus*.
- For each offence consider the following:

Actus reus	
Assault or battery	Did D cause someone to apprehend immediate personal harm (*Ireland*)?
	Was there an unlawful and direct application of force (*Thomas*)?
	Did any harm occur? If it did a more serious offence may have occurred.
	If so you should discuss **s 47**, but remember you will still need to discuss assault and/or battery as one of these is needed for **s 47**.
Assault occasioning actual bodily harm	**S 47** applies if harm has occurred following an assault (or battery).
	It includes most types of harm but the harm must be more than trivial – *Chan Fook*.
	Ireland confirmed the word 'assault' in **s 47** means common assault so includes either assault or battery.
	Enlarge on any **relevant** issues, referring to the given facts, e.g. harm can now include psychiatric harm (*Ireland/Burstow*), battery can be via another (*Haystead*).
	Discuss causation where this is an issue – was harm foreseeable? Did something happen that might break the chain of causation (*Roberts/Cheshire*)? Add the 'thin skull rule' if applicable – *Blaue*.
Unlawful and malicious wounding or inflicting/causing grievous bodily harm	Under **s 20** or **s 18** there must be a wound (*Eisenhower*) or serious harm (*Saunders*).
Mens rea	
Intent	It can be direct (D's aim or purpose) or indirect (*Nedrick/Woollin* – was the result a virtual certainty? Did D appreciate this?). This usually only needs discussing for **s 18**.
Subjective recklessness	D saw a risk and went ahead anyway – *Cunningham*.
	• *Mens rea* for **s 47** is intent or subjective recklessness as to the assault/battery, not the resulting harm – *Roberts/Savage*.
	• *Mens rea* for **s 20** is intent or subjective recklessness as to *some* harm, not serious harm – *Mowatt*.
	• *Mens rea* for **s 18** is intent (**only**) to cause serious harm (*Parmenter*) so you may only need to discuss this briefly to say why intent may not be proved and go on to **s 20** as an alternative.

Exam practice

AQA January 2010

Encouraged by their friends while they were all being rowdy, Henry and Jack took part in a 'boxing match' in which each had one glove and both wore blindfolds. During the match, Henry had struck Jack twice in the face, leaving him with red marks and a small swelling under his eye. Jack then took out a knife which he had hidden in his pocket. Before anyone could intervene, Jack lashed out in Henry's direction but missed him and, instead, inflicted a deep cut on the arm of Karim, one of the friends who was watching. The cut required a large number of stitches.

Consider the liability of Henry for the injuries to Jack, and the liability of Jack for the injuries to Karim.

[25 marks]

Answers online

Online

5 Defences

Introduction

The defences you need to revise for Unit 3A are insanity, automatism, intoxication, consent and self-defence. If you are studying crime for Unit 4A you will also need duress but that is dealt with in the next study block. Insanity and automatism overlap and are also known as insane automatism and non-insane automatism. The first is more often just called 'insanity' and is brought about by some kind of internal factor affecting the mind. The latter is more often just called 'automatism' and is brought about by an external factor. We'll look at the separate rules and then at the problems with both defences together.

Insanity Revised ☐

The rules on insanity come from the case of *M'Naghten (1843)*:

- Everyone is to be presumed to be sane.

- However, insanity may be proved if, at the time of committing the act D was:

  'labouring under such a defect of reason, from disease of the mind, as not to know the nature and quality of the act he was doing, or if he did know it, that he did not know he was doing what was wrong'.

There are thus four elements to revise:

- defect of reason
- disease of the mind
- not knowing the nature of the act
- not knowing it was wrong.

Defect of reason

- D must be unable to reason at the time of the offence.
- Temporary absentmindedness is not enough – *Clarke (1972)*.
- In *Clarke*, she absentmindedly took items from a supermarket while depressed; this was not insanity.

Disease of the mind

- The defect of reason must be caused by a disease of the mind.
- Disease of the mind is a legal concept to be decided by the judge.
- The courts have made a distinction between *internal* factors and *external* factors.
- The first will be insanity.
- The second will be automatism.

- In *Hennessey* (1983), a diabetic had taken a car and driven while disqualified. He had failed to take his insulin and this had caused him to lose control of his actions. He pleaded the defence of automatism. The court held that his failure to take insulin meant it was the diabetes which caused his defect of reason and this was an internal factor. The correct defence was insanity.
- In *Quick* (1973), a diabetic nurse at a psychiatric hospital attacked one of the patients. He had failed to eat after taking insulin and said this had caused him to lose control of his actions. The court held that his failure to eat meant that the insulin caused his loss of control and this was an external factor. This would therefore be automatism not insanity.
- In *Burgess* (1991), D claimed he was sleepwalking when he hit V over the head with a bottle. He argued automatism but the court held that the cause of his defect of reason was an internal factor so the defence was insanity.
- In *Kemp* (1956), D had a narrowing of the arteries which reduced the flow of blood to the brain. This caused lapses of consciousness. During one of these he attacked his wife with a hammer. His defence was treated as insanity.
- In *Sullivan* (1984), D hit out at someone during an epileptic fit and was convicted of ABH. The HL confirmed that the appropriate defence would be insanity and that epilepsy was a 'disease of the mind'.

Not knowing the nature of the act

The question is whether D understands the nature of the act which caused the offence.

- In *Burgess*, he did not know the nature of his actions because he was sleepwalking.
- In *Sullivan*, he did not understand what he was doing when he hit out during an epileptic fit, causing ABH.
- In *Kemp*, he did not understand the nature of what he was doing because of a lapse of consciousness.

Not knowing it was wrong

This means D not knowing the act is *legally* wrong.

Even if D has a defect of reason caused by a disease of the mind, if D knows that the act is legally wrong the defence fails.

In *Windle* (1952), D killed his wife with an overdose and then said 'I suppose they will hang me for this'.

This showed that he knew his actions were legally wrong.

In *Johnson* (2007), D forced his way into a neighbour's flat and stabbed him with a large kitchen knife. At his trial for wounding with intent, he said that he did not know what he was doing. The medical experts agreed that he had a disease of the mind, paranoid schizophrenia, but the judge said that he knew his actions were legally wrong so the defence failed.

Insanity and intoxication

If the defect of reason comes about through intoxication by drink or drugs, the defence fails.

In *Lipman* (1970), D had taken LSD and was hallucinating. He thought he was fighting snakes and killed his girlfriend by stuffing a sheet down her throat. He had a defect of reason and did not know the quality of his act. However, this was caused by the LSD so the defence failed.

If the defect of reason comes from alcoholism, it could succeed as this can be classed as a 'disease'.

Result of the defence succeeding

If the defence of insanity succeeds, the result is a special verdict of not guilty by reason of insanity and the judge gives an order as appropriate. The Criminal Procedure (Insanity and Unfitness to Plead) Act 1991 increased the powers a judge has and there are now four possible orders:

● a hospital order (indefinite or for a specified time)

● a guardianship order

● a supervisory treatment order

● an absolute discharge.

If the charge is murder, a hospital order is the only option.

Now test yourself

Tested

1 Add the principle and/or which defence applied in the following cases:

Case	Brief facts	Principle
Clarke (1972)	She absentmindedly took items from a supermarket shelf.	
Windle (1952)	D killed his wife with an overdose but his words showed he knew his actions were legally wrong.	
Kemp (1956)	D attacked his wife with a hammer due to a disease which reduced the flow of blood to the brain.	
Quick (1973)	A diabetic failed to eat after taking insulin and assaulted a patient.	
Hennessey (1983)	A diabetic failed to take his insulin and this had caused him to lose control of his actions.	
Sullivan (1984)	D hit out at someone during an epileptic fit.	
Burgess (1991)	D hit V over the head with a bottle when sleepwalking.	
Johnson (2007)	D forced his way into a neighbour's flat and stabbed him.	

Answers on page 120

Automatism

Revised

Remember from the introduction that you need to distinguish between insane automatism and non-insane automatism. It is fine to call the first insanity and the second automatism.

Automatism was defined in *Bratty v A-G for Northern Ireland (1963)* as an act 'done by the muscles without any control by the mind such as a spasm, a reflex action or a convulsion or an act done by a person who is not conscious of what he is doing ...'. D had killed a girl during an epileptic fit so this was insanity not automatism, but the definition has been used since.

The main points are:

● D had no control in that the act was involuntary.

● This was due to an external factor.

● If automatism was self-induced the defence fails.

D had no control

- The loss of control must be complete.
- In *Attorney-General's Reference (No 2 of 1992) (1994)*, D killed two people when his lorry crashed into a car on the hard shoulder of the motorway. He argued automatism but the evidence showed that he had some control over the vehicle at the time. The defence failed.

This was due to an external factor

- In *Hill v Baxter (1958)*, the court gave as an example a swarm of bees causing a driver to crash.
- Also look back at the cases on insanity.
- In *Quick*, the insulin was an external factor so the defence was automatism not insanity.

Automatism was self-induced

If D took drugs or drink and this caused the action the defence fails.

- In *Hardie (1984)*, D set fire to a bedroom after taking Valium. A distinction was made between drugs supposed to calm and unpredictable drugs.
- The defence failed in *Lipman*, because he voluntarily took LSD and this is known to be unpredictable.
- In *Bailey (1983)*, a diabetic had failed to eat and hit a man over the head with an iron bar. He argued automatism but the CA held he had not lost total control and also restated that self-induced automatism would not usually be acceptable.

Now test yourself

Tested

2 Add the brief facts and principle and/or which defence applied in the following cases:

Case	Brief facts	Principle
Bratty (1963)		
Lipman (1970)		
Bailey (1983)		
Hardie (1984)		
A-G's Reference (No 2 of 1992) (1994)		

Answers on page 120

Consequence

A successful defence of automatism leads to an acquittal.

Exam tip

There is an overlap with insanity so you may need to discuss both. Automatism should be the preferred option if it applies as this leads to a complete acquittal, but remember to highlight the internal/external nature of the cause.

Points for an essay on problems and proposals for reform – insanity and automatism

- The defence of insanity originates from an 1843 case and medical advances since then mean it should be updated.
- The 1953 Royal Commission on Capital Punishment recommended the abolition of the *M'Naghten* rules.
- The Homicide Act 1957 (now itself amended by the Coroners and Justice Act) introduced diminished responsibility shortly after this which addressed some of the criticisms.
- There is an overlap with diminished responsibility but both have the stigma of being shown to be mentally unsound.
- The burden of proof is on the defendant.
- In 1975, the Butler Committee recommended a new verdict of 'not guilty by reason of mental disorder'. Also, that the burden of proof should move to the prosecution.
- The Law Commission's Draft Code 1989 adopted many of Butler's recommendations and also suggested that sleepwalking and spasms should come within automatism not insanity.
- The Commission made some further recommendations in 1995 but these were not acted upon.
- In their 2012 scoping paper, the LC noted that the law lagged behind psychiatric understanding (for more on this see 'Check your understanding: 1' below).
- The rules on insanity and automatism have led to sleepwalkers, epileptics and diabetics being labelled insane, which seems unjust.
- The difference between not taking insulin (insanity), and taking it but not eating properly (automatism), is small but the different consequence is that D is found insane or goes free.

Check your understanding: 1 Insanity and automatism

Go to the Law Commission website (**www.justice.gov.uk/lawcommission/areas/insanity.htm**) and look at what they say about insanity and automatism in the introduction to their 2012 scoping paper, then answer the questions below.

1 What is the essence of the insanity offence?

2 What is the essence of the automatism defence?

3 What four main criticisms are highlighted?

4 Are there many successful insanity pleas?

Answers on page 120

Intoxication

Revised

Intoxication rarely succeeds as a defence but may do if it negates *mens rea*.

In *Dowds* (see under 'Diminished responsibility' on page 18), the CA stated that the rules on intoxication apply to all defences, and to intoxication caused by drugs or other substances as well as alcohol.

Case example

In *Lipman* (see 'Insanity' on page 37), he had taken drugs and so had no *mens rea* for murder (no intent), but was guilty of manslaughter instead.

The main issues to consider are:

● whether the crime was one of specific or basic intent
● whether intoxication was voluntary or involuntary.

Specific or basic intent

This distinction was made in *Majewski (1976)*:

● Essentially a specific intent crime is one where the *mens rea* is intent only.
● Examples in Unit 3 are murder and **s 18 OAPA**.
● A case example is *Lipman* (see the previous page) where he had taken drugs and so had no *mens rea* for murder (a specific intent crime), but was guilty of manslaughter (a basic intent crime).
● Essentially a basic intent offence is one where the *mens rea* includes recklessness.
● Examples in Unit 3 are manslaughter (involuntary) and the other non-fatal offences.
● A case example is *Majewski* itself where he had taken drink and drugs when he committed ABH:
  – The court held his intoxication was no defence.
  – The *mens rea* for ABH includes recklessness.
  – D is seen as reckless in getting intoxicated so has *mens rea* for the basic intent crime.

Even in a specific intent crime intoxication only succeeds if it negates *mens rea*.

In *A-G for Northern Ireland v Gallagher (1963)*, D bought a knife to kill his wife and a bottle of whisky to give himself 'Dutch courage'. The court held that a drunken intent is still intent and rejected the defence. He had intent to kill so was guilty of murder.

Voluntary intoxication

Using the above cases you can see the effect of voluntary intoxication in both specific and basic intent crimes.

● In *Lipman*, he was charged with a specific intent crime (murder) but was guilty of manslaughter instead.
● This shows that for specific intent crimes even if the *mens rea* of intent is not there, there is still recklessness in voluntarily taking unpredictable drugs so the result is a manslaughter conviction.
● In *Majewski*, he was guilty of ABH and the defence could not be used because this is a basic intent crime.
● This shows that for basic intent crimes D will not be able to use the defence at all if the intoxication was voluntary.

Involuntary intoxication

● This may succeed for both specific and basic intent crimes. It may occur where D's coffee or soft drink were laced with alcohol or D took prescribed drugs but they had an unexpected effect.
● In *Kingston (1994)*, D's coffee was laced with drugs. He then abused a young boy and was charged with indecent assault. He argued that he would not have done this had he not been drugged. The HL held:

- To succeed the intoxication must negate the *mens rea*.
- The fact that it removed inhibitions and he wouldn't have done it if sober is not enough.
- Kingston intended to commit the offence, so he had *mens rea*.

- In *Hardie* (see 'Automatism' on page 39), he was not reckless as he did not know the effects of the drug which was supposed to calm him.
- This can be compared to *Lipman* and *Majewski* where the effect of the drugs and drink were known to be unpredictable.

> **Exam tip**
>
> The defences of insanity, automatism and intoxication overlap so you may well need to discuss all three if, for example the facts show that D has taken drugs and these have affected his mind. The next 'Check your understanding' shows this.

Check your understanding: 2 Application practice

5 Using the case of *Lipman*, apply the law on insanity, automatism and intoxication to the facts and come to a conclusion as to which defence to a murder charge is most likely to succeed, if any.

Answers on pages 120–21

> **Exam tip**
>
> In a case like *Lipman*, you could also discuss the possible defence of diminished responsibility as this applies to a murder charge. You were only asked to discuss the three particular defences in the previous exercise but note that in an examination, once you have applied the defence(s) and decided it is not murder, you would then need to go on to apply the rules on unlawful act manslaughter.

Points for an essay on problems with intoxication

- The ruling in *Majewski* suggests that being drunk is reckless enough behaviour to provide the *mens rea* for a basic intent crime, which seems unfair.
- It is hard to argue that D has *mens rea* when clearly not in control due to intoxication, but the defence will fail if the intoxication was voluntary.
- If there is no *mens rea* for the particular crime, the normal legal principle is that there is no liability. This has given way to public policy – that intoxication should not excuse a criminal act.

Key cases on intoxication

Case	Brief facts	Principle
A-G for Northern Ireland v Gallagher (1963)	D killed his wife having bought a knife and some whisky.	A drunken intent is still intent.
Majewski (1976)	D hit someone while drunk.	Intoxication is not a defence to basic intent crimes, only those of specific intent.
Kingston (1994)	D's coffee was laced and he committed an indecent assault.	If D has *mens rea* the defence fails even if the intoxication was involuntary.
Dowds (2012)	D had been drinking when he attacked and killed his partner.	The rules on intoxication apply to all defences, and to intoxication caused by drugs or other substances as well as alcohol.

Striving for an A/A*?

Look at the Law Commission's scoping paper on insanity and automatism (see 'Check your understanding: 1' on page 40 for the link) and download the PDF file. Do the same for intoxication (look under 'intoxication' in the 'A–Z of projects'). Quotations and comments from these reports will greatly enhance an essay.

Self-defence

There are two defences which come under the heading of self-defence:

- self-defence (which includes defence of another) at common law, and
- prevention of crime under the Criminal Law Act 1967.

The same rules apply for both:

- In both cases the defence is only available if the force used is 'reasonable in the circumstances'.
- **S 76** Criminal Justice and Immigration Act 2008 applies to both and provides that 'a person may use such force as is reasonable in the circumstances'.

The force used is 'reasonable in the circumstances'

Case example

In *Martin*, the farmer shot and killed a burglar and seriously injured another. The jury rejected self-defence as they were retreating and there was clearly no threat, so using a pump-action shotgun was not reasonable force in the circumstances.

S 76 explains the degree of force which can be used:

- D 'may not be able to weigh to a nicety the exact measure of any necessary action'.
- If D only did what was 'honestly and instinctively thought' to be necessary this would be 'strong evidence that only reasonable action was taken'.
- Whether force is reasonable is decided by reference 'to the circumstances as D believed them to be'.
- This is based on *Williams (Gladstone) (1987)*.

Case example

In *Williams*, D punched a police officer whom he thought was assaulting someone and was charged with ABH. The court held that he was to be judged on the facts as he saw them and his defence succeeded.

- So if D mistakenly believes someone is being assaulted then self-defence may be relied on even if there was no actual assault.
- **S 76** confirms this by stating that whether force is reasonable is decided by reference 'to the circumstances as D believed them to be'.
- This applies even if the mistake is unreasonable as long as genuinely held.
- **S 76** states that the mistake need not be reasonable, but the more reasonable it is, the more likely it was genuinely held.

Now test yourself

3   Why was self-defence rejected by the jury in *Martin*?
4   Can you rely on a mistaken belief to justify using force?
5   Use a case in support of the above answer.
6   Can you rely on an intoxicated mistake?
7   Use a case in support of the above answer.
8   What is the result of a successful plea of self-defence?

Answers on page 121

Other elements of the defence

- D does not have to wait until attacked before using force.

- In *A-G's Reference (No 2 of 1983)*, D prepared petrol bombs in fear of an attack on his shop and the CA accepted that D could make advance preparations in self-defence.

- Under **s 76 (5)** D cannot rely on a mistaken belief caused by voluntary intoxication.

- This confirms *O'Grady (1987)*, where D hit a friend over the head in the mistaken belief that the friend was trying to kill him and the defence was rejected.

- If force is excessive the defence fails.

Case example

In *Martin* (see the previous page), the CA confirmed that the farmer was entitled to use reasonable force to protect himself and his home, but agreed with the jury that the force was excessive.

Check your understanding: 3 Application practice for self-defence

6 You are walking down the street one night when you see a man come towards you with a gun. You believe you are being attacked and throw a brick at him. It turns out he was coming to ask you for directions and he was only holding a torch. You are charged with causing grievous bodily harm. State your defence.

7 Walking home from college you see a woman assaulting a young boy. You intervene and pull her away but she trips and is badly bruised. You are charged with actual bodily harm. State your defence.

Answers on page 121

Summary

There are essentially two questions on self-defence for the jury:

- ✔ Did D genuinely believe force was necessary in the circumstances? (What D believed; a subjective question.)
  - A case example is *Williams*.
- ✔ Was the degree of force reasonable in those circumstances? (What a normal person would see as reasonable; an objective question.)
  - A case example is *Martin*.
- ✔ D can rely on an unreasonable mistake as long as genuinely held – *Williams*/**s 76.**
- ✔ D cannot rely on a drunken mistake – *O'Grady*/**s 76.**

Consent

Revised

This defence is mainly relevant to the non-fatal offences against the person. The main points are:

- Consent must be real.
- Consent may be implied.
- Whether the defence is accepted depends on the level of injury.
- Consent is never a defence to murder.

Consent must be real

In *Tabassum (2000)*, D said he was preparing a database for doctors and persuaded several women to allow him to measure their breasts. They knew the nature of the action he planned to take but said they only consented because they thought he was a doctor. The CA approved the decision of the trial judge that consent to a medical examination was not the same as consent to indecent behaviour; the act consented to was not the act done so the defence failed.

In *Dica (2004)*, D had sex with two women knowing that he was HIV positive, and they both became infected with HIV. He was convicted of GBH. He argued that they had consented but the defence was rejected. On appeal the CA said that there had to be consent to the risk of harm, not just consent to sex.

Consent may be implied

In *A-G's Reference (No 6 of 1980) (1981)*, two youths agreed to have a fight in the street and one of them was charged with ABH. The CA held that it was not in the public interest that people should cause each other bodily harm for no good reason. The defence failed but the CA went on to give a list of circumstances where it might succeed even if harm is caused. These included:

- properly conducted games and sports
- lawful chastisement or correction
- reasonable surgical interference.

In these circumstances, consent is implied even if injury is caused.

Properly conducted games and sports

- In *Billingshurst (1978)*, consent was accepted even though the injury suffered was serious and D was acting outside the rules of rugby.
- In *Barnes (2004)*, D was convicted of GBH after a late tackle in a football match. On appeal the CA held that criminal cases should be reserved for times when the conduct was 'sufficiently grave to be categorised as criminal' and quashed the conviction.
- Implied consent is also accepted for 'rough horseplay'.
- In *Jones (1988)*, a group of boys tossed two other boys into the air causing serious injuries and the defence was allowed.
- In *Aitken (1992)*, drunken RAF officers doused another officer with white spirit and set fire to him. The court held that there was implied consent to 'rough and undisciplined horseplay'.

Lawful chastisement or correction

- Corporal punishment in schools has been illegal since 1986.
- Parents smacking their own children was excluded from this law.
- Under the Children Act 2004, smacking by a parent is illegal where it causes bruising or cuts.
- However, consent will still be a defence to common assault (assault or battery).

Reasonable surgical interference

- Most surgical operations will involve some kind of injury by their very nature.

> **Exam tip**
>
> As with self-defence, there are two ways to approach a scenario where someone appears to have consented to D's act. Consent can, for example, make a battery lawful. This means part of the *actus reus* is not proved so you can argue that there is no offence. Alternatively you can say that if charged with battery D can use the defence of consent and explain the rules on this defence. Either approach is acceptable.

- We saw in *Tabassum* that there must be real consent to surgical interference.
- This can be compared to *Richardson (1999)*, where a dentist who had been suspended carried out treatment on several people. It was argued that consent was not real because the patients did not know he had been suspended. The CA held that they had consented to the treatment, and this was enough.
- Age may be relevant. In *Burrell and Harmer (1967)*, a twelve- and thirteen-year-old were caused ABH when they got tattoos done. They were not deemed to have consented.

Whether the defence is accepted depends on the level of injury

- Although consent is available as a defence to assault it is less likely to succeed where injury is caused.
- Partly this is for public policy reasons. As we saw in *A-G's Reference (No 6 of 1980) (1981)*, the CA held that it was not in the public interest that people should cause each other bodily harm for no good reason.
- In *Brown (1994)*, all the victims consented to sado-masochistic activities which caused serious harm. The defence failed in respect of both the ABH and the GBH charges.
- It now seems that consent will not be allowed if injury results unless one of the above exceptions applies.
- In *Barnes*, the CA confirmed that sporting activities were an exception to the rule that consent is not a defence where bodily harm occurs.
- However, the CA also said that if injury was inflicted intentionally the defence will fail.
- Cases are not always consistent. In *Wilson (1996)*, a man branded his initials on his wife's buttocks and the injuries were severe enough to need medical treatment. It was clearly intentional but the defence succeeded.

Consent is never a defence where death is caused

This was confirmed in *Pretty (2001)*, where a woman wanted her husband to help her to die. She wanted to choose the time of her death because she had an incurable disease, but was physically incapable of taking her own life. She was fully aware of the facts so there was real consent, but the HL refused her argument and held that if her husband assisted her it would be a criminal act.

Points for an essay on problems with consent

- The situations in *Jones* and in *Aitken* seem more like violent bullying than 'horseplay' but the defence of consent was accepted.
- It can be argued that it is inconsistent to allow consent in cases like *Aitken* and not in cases like *Brown* where there was real consent.
- It appears from *Barnes* that consent is a defence to reckless harm, but not to intentional harm.
- However, cases have not been consistent on this issue as the harm was intentional in *Wilson*.
- Arguably, Parliament should legislate on the issue of consent.

Exam practice answers and quick quizzes at **www.therevisionbutton.co.uk/myrevisionnotes**

Key cases on consent

Case	Brief facts	Principle
Tabassum (2000)	Women consented to a medical examination.	There must be true consent or the defence fails.
Barnes (2004)	A football tackle caused serious injury.	Consent is implied in sports unless the act was grave enough to be criminal.
A-G's Reference (No 6 of 1980) (1981)	A fight between two youths in the street occurred.	The CA gave guidance on activities where consent would be implied.
Burrell and Harmer (1967)	Young boys were tattooed which caused injury.	Age may be relevant to whether consent is implied.
Pretty (2001)	A woman wishing to be helped to die.	Consent is never a defence to a death.

Exam tip

Learn the main points for each of the defences with the cases that set out any key principles plus one or two other cases so you can more easily identify the most appropriate defence based on the factual situations in the examination scenario. Refer to the facts in the scenario as you apply the law to show the examiner you have picked out the key points.

Typical mistake

Many students forget to deal with defences at all. It is easy to forget things in the stress of an examination so be sure to remember this and look carefully at the facts to identify if there is a possible defence.

Check your understanding: 4 Application practice for consent

Apply the defence of consent to the following situations to decide if it is likely to succeed or fail. The charge is given in brackets to give you a hint.

8 Jack tackled and was sent off for foul play (GBH **s 20 OAPA**).

9 Lita got a serious infection after Tom gave her nose piercings (ABH).

10 Diane begged her husband to help her end her life (assisted suicide or murder).

Answers on page 121

Summary

These are the key cases of all defences.

Defence	Main points	Case	Effect
Insanity	There must be a defect of reason caused by disease of the mind.	*M'Naghten (1843)* rules	Not guilty by reason of insanity.
Automatism	There must be a total loss of control (caused by an external factor).	*A-G's Reference No 2*	Acquittal.
Intoxication – involuntary	Intoxication must remove *mens rea*.	*Kingston (1994)*	Acquittal.
Intoxication – voluntary	May remove *mens rea* of intent but not recklessness.	*Majewski (1976)*	D guilty of the associated basic intent crime.
Self-defence	Force must be reasonable.	*Martin (2001)*	Acquittal.
	Judged on the facts as D believes them.	*Williams (1992)*	
	Any mistake must be genuine but need not be reasonable.	*Williams (1992)*	
Consent	Consent must be real.	*Richardson (1999)*	Acquittal.
	Consent can be implied.	*A-G's Reference No 6*	

Exam practice

AQA January 2011

Write a critical analysis of any two of the general defences (insanity, automatism, intoxication, consent, self-defence/prevention of crime). Include in your answer a consideration of any proposals for reform of one of your chosen defences.

[25 marks]

Answers online

Online

Exam tip

You will see that you only have to deal with two defences and this will always be the case. This means you can concentrate on the two you feel most comfortable with but be sure you know the main criticisms and learn several cases to support a critique of your chosen defences.

Unit 4 Section A: Criminal Law (Offences against the Property)

Introduction

This unit is divided into six chapters covering:

- theft and robbery
- burglary
- blackmail
- fraud and making off without payment
- criminal damage
- defences.

Theft and robbery go together (robbery requires theft to be proved first) so are included in one chapter. This makes the first section much longer than the second, which only covers burglary, so bear this in mind when planning your revision. Chapter 6 (pages 51–57) can be split up into theft AR, theft MR and robbery so that you revise one area and do the exercises within that before going on to the next.

Note that there is no evaluation for any of Unit 4A because that comes in Unit 4C: Concepts of Law. Therefore there are no 'Points for an essay' and no essay practice.

The problem scenarios for this area are likely to cover a wide range of the offences in Unit 4A. All the previous papers since 2010 have mixed several offences in each paper, therefore the examination questions are found at the end of the last chapter on defences. Note that the scenarios at this level are more complex and you will need to have a sound knowledge of cases and Acts of Parliament to support your application of the law.

The examination

- Examinations take place once a year in June. (The last January exams were in 2013.)
- The exam lasts for 2 hours and you are advised to spend no more than 1 hour on this unit (the remaining hour is for Unit 4C).
- You can choose one scenario from two on the law you have studied for this unit.
- Both questions will be asking you to apply the relevant law to the scenario given.
- You must answer both questions on the scenario you choose.
- Each question is worth 25 marks.
- Each question carries 10 marks for AO1 and 15 marks for AO2.

Help from the exam board

- The AQA website has a lot of important and useful information and guidance. It tells you what you need to cover in each topic and explains the Assessment Objectives (AO1, AO2 and AO3).

- There are plenty of past examination papers, together with mark schemes and examiners' reports.

- It is important to look at these for revision because they give you helpful guidance on what should be covered in order to reach the higher grades.

Preparing for the exam

- You need to be prepared to answer questions on all the topics in the unit. The material in this Revision Guide will help you do this, but you should also look at previous papers, mark schemes and reports to prepare properly for the exam.

- To gain high marks, answers need to be relevant to the question asked. It is important to be selective and not just to write down all you know about an area. This approach does not gain marks because it indicates that you do not know how to apply the *relevant* law.

- The level of detail needed will depend on how many areas of law are covered. Where there are several areas to be covered, less detail will be expected.

- You should revise the material thoroughly, so that you go into the exam with confidence.

- You need to understand the law, not just to be able to reproduce it. You will need to adapt it to answer questions that are slightly different from those that you may have answered before.

- You should practise answering questions under exam conditions so you can learn to manage your time efficiently.

Use of authorities

- You will need to refer to authorities in support of your answer; these include examples, cases and Acts of Parliament.

- For cases, the date of the case is not important and with long or complicated case names it is sufficient to use a shortened version. Examiners will know which case you mean. Criminal cases are usually written *R v*, but in most law textbooks (including this Revision Guide) the cases are referred to by the name of the defendant only.

- For Acts of Parliament, it is important to include the date and to know the different section numbers for the different parts of the *actus reus* and *mens rea*.

6 Theft and robbery

Introduction

This chapter covers both theft and robbery. This is because theft is needed before a robbery can be proved. Essentially theft is stealing something, and robbery is where this is done with the use of violence, or the threat of violence.

Theft

Under **s 1 (1)** Theft Act 1968, a person is guilty of theft:

> 'if he dishonestly appropriates property belonging to another with the intention of permanently depriving the other of it'.

Look through this definition and see if you can pick out the *actus reus* and *mens rea* and then check your answer in the table below.

- **S1** defines theft then each part of the *actus reus* and *mens rea* is further explained in **s 2–s 6**.
- The charge of theft therefore comes under **s 1** only.

Actus reus	Mens rea
Appropriation **s 3**	Dishonesty **s 2**
Of property **s 4**	Intention permanently to deprive **s 6**
Belonging to another **s 5**	

Exam tip

You need to know these five sections and to be able to cite case examples of each so that you can apply the correct law to the facts of a given scenario.

We'll take each in turn.

Appropriation s 3   Revised

- This is defined in **s 3 (1)** as 'any assumption by a person of the rights of an owner'.
- This is very wide because an owner has a right to do most things, e.g. sell, rent, or even destroy the property.
- A person has appropriated the property if that person does any of these things because the owner's rights have been 'assumed'.
- In *Morris (1983)*, swapping price labels in a supermarket for lower ones before putting the items in a basket was appropriation.
- The HL held appropriation was interference with any of the rights of the owner and added that there must be an adverse interference with the owner's rights.

What if the owner consents to the appropriation?

- In *Morris*, the HL held there must be an adverse, or unauthorised, appropriation.
- This conflicted with the earlier decision in *Lawrence (1972)*.
- In *Lawrence*, the student had offered the taxi-driver his wallet to take the fare from and it was held to be theft when he took too much.

- In *Morris*, the owner would consent to taking goods off the supermarket shelf, but not to switching labels so it was at the later point that appropriation occurred.
- *Lawrence* was preferred and followed in *Gomez (1993)* where an assistant manager of a shop persuaded his boss to accept stolen cheques from a friend for goods.
- The CA quashed his conviction because the manager had consented.
- The HL held there was no need for an adverse interference with the owner's rights and reinstated the conviction.
- So an appropriation can take place even where the owner consents.
- *Lawrence* was followed again in *Hinks (2000)*, where a man with a low IQ had gone further than consent and had actually given money and a television to a woman who claimed to be his carer.
- The HL held there was an appropriation even though there was a legal gift of the property.
- However, consent may be relevant when deciding if D is dishonest (see MR on pages 54–55).

What if the property is acquired innocently?

- **S 3 (1)** continues with 'and this includes, where he has come by the property (innocently or not) without stealing it, any later assumption of a right to it by keeping or dealing with it as owner'.
- Thus if something is acquired innocently it can be appropriated later by 'keeping' or 'dealing with' it.

Example

If you picked up a mobile phone, thinking it was yours, there is no appropriation. However, if you decide to keep it or sell it once you realise your mistake that will be appropriation.

Property s 4

Revised

- Under **s 4 (1)** property includes: 'money and all other property, real or personal, including things in action and other intangible property'.
- Real property relates to land, personal property is anything else.
- 'Things in action' are so called because they can only be enforced by a court action.
- Other intangible property is something you cannot touch, such as the copyright of song lyrics or a bank balance.
- Body parts can come within **s 4** if they have been treated in some way, e.g. by dissecting or preserving them for medical purposes – *Kelly and Lindsay (1998)*.

In *Oxford v Moss (1979)*, an examination paper was taken but it was not theft because he intended to return it, so just wanted knowledge of the questions, and this was not property.

- **S 4 (3)** excludes mushrooms and plants growing wild, unless taken for 'reward or sale or other commercial purpose'.
- **S 4 (4)** excludes wild creatures, unless they have been tamed or kept in captivity.

Typical mistake

An issue which commonly arises in problem questions and which many students fail to understand, is that it can be theft even if D doesn't take anything. This is because appropriation occurs as soon as one of the owner's rights is assumed. As long as all the other elements are also proved this would be theft – so in *Morris*, the theft occurred once labels were swapped, and since *Gomez*, it would be at the time of removing them from the shelf.

Exam tip

Note that *Gomez* followed *Lawrence*, so appropriation now occurs at the time the goods are taken off the shelf. It may be hard to prove all the elements of theft, especially *mens rea*, before reaching the checkout but you should be clear at which point appropriation has occurred, because if they can be proved then theft occurs at this point.

Exam tip

Note the exceptions here, as these are common examination issues. Watch for clues such as 'D picked some **wild** garlic and **sold** it to …'. The word 'wild' directs you to **s 4 (3)** that wild plants can't normally be stolen because they are not 'property' but the word 'sold' directs you to the exception where they are taken for 'reward or sale or other commercial purpose'.

Belonging to another s 5 — Revised

S 5 (1) provides that 'Property shall be regarded as belonging to any person having possession or control of it, or having in it any proprietary right or interest ...'.

- It is possible to steal your own property if it is under someone else's possession or control, or someone else has a legal interest in it – *Turner (1971)*.

- It is possible to possess or control property even if you don't know the property is there – *Woodman (1974)*.

Obligation to deal with the property in a certain way

Under **s 5 (3)** where someone receives property from another and there is an obligation to deal with that property in a particular way:

- The property or proceeds shall be regarded as belonging to the other.

- This means if something is given for a purpose, not using it for that purpose can be theft.

> **Example**
>
> Your mother gives you £20 and asks you to do the shopping tomorrow. You received property, the £20. You are obliged to retain it until tomorrow, and to deal with it by doing the shopping. You may have been given the £20, but under **s 5 (3)** it is property belonging to your mother.

> **Case example**
>
> In *Davidge v Bunnett (1984)*, a girl given money by flatmates to pay bills had an obligation to pay the bills. When she bought Christmas presents instead this was theft.

- There must be an obligation to retain or deal with the property 'in a particular way'.

- Therefore, it was not theft in *Hall (1973)*, where a travel agent paid deposits for flights into his firm's account and was later unable to repay the money. There had been no special arrangements for the deposits to be used in a particular way.

Property received by mistake

- Under **s 5 (4)**, if you are given something by mistake (and so have an obligation to give it back) the property is treated as still belonging to the other person.

- An example would be being overpaid wages by mistake. You have an obligation to return that amount, so keeping it can be theft.

- This happened in *A-G's Reference (No 1 of 1983)*.

> **Now test yourself** — Tested
>
> 1 When can wild plants be classed as property?
> 2 When can animals be classed as property?
> 3 Did *Gomez* follow *Morris* or *Lawrence* on the issue of consent?
> 4 What was appropriated in *Hinks*?
> 5 Why was the girl guilty of theft in *Davidge v Bunnett*?
> 6 Why was the travel agent not guilty of theft in *Hall*?
>
> **Answers on page 121**

Key cases

Brief facts	Principle	Case name
D switched labels on goods in a supermarket.	Appropriation is an adverse interference with goods.	*Morris (1983)*
D knew she'd been overpaid but left the money in her bank account.	Keeping property received by mistake can be theft because there is an obligation to return it.	*A-G's Reference (No 1 of 1983)*
D took some body parts from the Royal College of Surgeons.	Body parts can be 'property' if they have been changed in some way.	*Kelly and Lindsay (1998)*
D took the 'knowledge' from an exam paper.	Knowledge is not 'property'.	*Oxford v Moss (1979)*
D took some leftover scrap metal.	A person can have possession or control without knowing the property exists.	*Woodman (1974)*
D was given money and a television.	Appropriation can occur even if the owner has given the property away.	*Hinks (2000)*
D spent the money given to her to pay bills on Christmas presents.	If there is an obligation to deal with property in a particular way, not doing so can be theft.	*Davidge v Bunnett (1984)*
D took his own car back without paying for the repairs.	It is possible to steal your own property if someone else has possession or control.	*Turner (1971)*
D persuaded the manager of a shop to accept stolen cheques in return for the goods.	Appropriation can occur even if the owner consents.	*Gomez (1993)*

That's AR revised – now the two MR issues.

Dishonesty s 2   Revised ☐

The Act does not define dishonesty but it provides that it is not deemed dishonest if a person:

- 'appropriates the property in the belief that he has in law the right to deprive the other of it, on behalf of himself or a third person' – **s 2 (1) (a)**

- 'appropriates the property in the belief that he would have the other's consent if the other knew of the appropriation and the circumstances of it' – **s 2 (1) (b)**

- 'appropriates the property in the belief that the person to whom the property belongs cannot be discovered by taking reasonable steps' – **s 2 (1) (c)**.

Example

You take a bicycle which belongs to a friend. You could argue under **s 2 (1) (a)** that the friend owed you money so you believed you had a legal right to take it. Alternatively you could argue under **s 2 (1) (b)** that you believed the friend would have consented in the circumstances. Under **s 2 (1) (c)** you could argue that you thought the friend had left the country and so couldn't be traced by taking reasonable steps.

- A case example is *Small (1987)*. D had taken a car which had been left for over a week with the keys in the ignition and argued it had been abandoned and so he believed he had a right to take it – **s 2 (1) (a)**. The CA quashed his conviction.

- The CA made clear that the issue under **s 2** is whether a belief is *honestly* held, not whether it is reasonable.

- It would be harder to argue a belief under **s 2 (1) (c)**, that the owner couldn't be traced, because it is easy to trace the owner of a car as it has to be registered.

- However, if someone was young or not very bright it may be easier to show an honest belief even if other people would think it unreasonable.

- This makes it a subjective test – what D believes.

Typical mistake

S 2 relates to *mens rea* not *actus reus*. Many students mistakenly say that D must take reasonable steps to find the owner. This is not the case. A *belief* that D could not trace the owner by taking reasonable steps would be sufficient; D does not have actually to take those steps.

Exam practice answers and quick quizzes at **www.therevisionbutton.co.uk/myrevisionnotes**

A test for dishonesty has been produced by case law. It comes from the case of *Ghosh (1982)* so is known as the 'Ghosh test'. D had claimed fees for an operation he had not done because he was owed other fees. The CA said there are two questions for the jury:

- Was D's act dishonest by the ordinary standards of reasonable and honest people? If not, stop here. If so, ask the second question:
- Did D realise the act would be regarded as dishonest by such people?

If the jury can answer 'yes' to both parts, D is dishonest.

Finally on dishonesty, **s 2 (2)** provides that the fact that you are willing to pay for the property does not mean you are acting honestly.

> **Exam tip**
>
> When discussing the *mens rea* of theft you may need to look at both **s 2** and *Ghosh*. Look for clues in the scenario set, e.g. any reference to being owed money should point you to **s 2 (1) (a)**, taking from a friend or colleague to **s 2 (1) (b)**, something found to **s 2 (1) (c)**. Reference to D's age or mental capacity requires you to discuss that it is what D believes that is important, not what is reasonable. If these don't apply, or may not succeed, then discuss and apply the *Ghosh* test.

Intention to permanently deprive s 6   Revised

- This is an 'intention is to treat the property as his own to dispose of regardless of the other's rights'.
- In *Velumyl (1989)*, D took money from his employer's safe, intending to return it. The CA held that this was sufficient, as he had treated the money as his own.
- In *Lavender (1994)*, D took some doors from his flat which belonged to the council. He hung them in his girlfriend's flat which belonged to the same council. Arguably, he hadn't intended permanently to deprive the council of the doors as he merely moved them. The court held D had treated the doors as his own.
- In *Raphael (2008)* (see Robbery on page 56), taking a car and demanding money for its return showed a clear 'intention to treat the property as his own to dispose of regardless of the other's rights'.
- The intention permanently to deprive will also exist where property is borrowed 'for a period and in circumstances making it equivalent to an outright taking or disposal'.

> **Example**
>
> You borrow a month's season ticket intending to return it later. You use it for three weeks and are charged with theft. You can argue that you had no intention permanently to deprive the owner of it. This argument is likely to fail. The use of it for three weeks out of the month will make it 'equivalent to an outright taking' and so comes within **s 6**.

> **Exam tip**
>
> If given a scenario like *Velumyl* you could argue that D may not be dishonest under **s 2**. Suggest D may have believed that the owner would have consented (perhaps borrowing from the employer had been allowed before), or D believed they had a right to it (perhaps they were owed wages). Alternatively rely on the *Ghosh* test. The jury may consider that by intending to return the money, D was not dishonest by ordinary standards.

- In *Lloyd (1985)*, D borrowed some films from the cinema where he worked and copied them. The CA held **s 6** applied if D used something so that 'all the goodness or virtue is gone'. This was not the case so there was no liability.

Check your understanding: 1

1 Look at the following scenarios to decide what in particular should be addressed concerning the *mens rea* of theft. A man takes a bicycle …

    a) and rides it to the shops, returning it an hour later.

    b) from his flatmate so he won't miss his train and be late for work.

    c) because he is owed more than the bike is worth by the owner.

    d) because he thinks it has been abandoned.

Answers on page 121

Now test yourself

7   Add the case, relevant part of the AR and principle to the facts in the table. The first is done for you as an example.

Brief facts	Principle	Case name and section
D switched labels on goods in a supermarket.	Appropriation can be any adverse interference with property.	*Morris* **s 3**
D knew she'd been overpaid but left the money in her bank account.		
D took some body parts from the Royal College of Surgeons.		
D took the 'knowledge' from an exam paper.		
D took some leftover scrap metal.		
D was given money and a television.		
D spent the money given to her to pay bills on Christmas presents.		
D took his own car back without paying for the repairs.		
D persuaded the manager of a shop to accept stolen cheques in return for the goods.		
D took some doors from his council flat.		
D took an abandoned car.		
D took a film from the cinema where he worked and copied it.		
D took money from the office safe.		

Answers on page 122

Summary

Actus reus			Mens rea	
Appropriation s 3	**Property s 4**	**Belonging to another s 5**	**Dishonesty s 2**	**Intent to permanently deprive s 6**
Even if with owner's consent – *Gomez*	Money and all other property Note the exceptions	Includes those with possession or control	**S 2** and/or *Ghosh* test	Can include borrowing

Robbery

- It is a more serious offence if D uses force (or the threat of force) in order to steal.

- **S (8) (1)** of the Theft Act 1968 provides:

  'A person is guilty of robbery if he steals, and **immediately before or at the time of doing so, and in order to do so, he uses force on any person or puts or seeks to put any person in fear of being then and there subjected to force**.'

The main elements

- Theft (**all** the elements of theft must be proved)
- plus force or the threat of it
- immediately before or at the time of the theft
- in order to steal.

Key cases including these elements

Case	Brief facts	Robbery issue
Robinson (1977)	D threatened V with a knife in order to get money he was owed.	He believed he had a legal right to the money so had a defence under **s 2 (1)**. There was no theft so no robbery.
Corcoran v Anderton (1980)	Ds snatched a bag from someone's grasp and dropped it.	This was sufficient force for a robbery and even though they ran off without the bag, there was a completed theft.
Clouden (1987)	Ds wrenched a shopping basket from someone's hand.	Even though the force was small it was sufficient to make it robbery.
Hale (1979)	One D took some property and the other tied the householder up.	Appropriation can be a continuing act; as it continued while the victim was tied up the force was 'in order to steal'.
Lockley (1995)	The Ds took some beer and used force on the shopkeeper in order to escape.	Confirming *Hale* the appropriation was seen as continuing.
Raphael (2008)	D took a car by force and then demanded payment for it to be returned.	**S 6 (1)** includes an intention to 'treat the thing as his own to dispose of regardless of the other's rights', and the demand for money clearly satisfied this. There was therefore a theft and the force used made it robbery.

Typical mistake

Where the scenario shows evidence of force being used in order to steal, too many students rush straight into robbery and a discussion of force and immediacy. The first thing that needs proving, however, is that a theft occurred, because if it has not then there cannot be a robbery.

Exam tip

If you have a scenario which appears to be a robbery because there is evidence of force, go through all the elements of theft first, dealing in more detail with any that are in doubt. Once you have proved theft, go on to **s 8** and the additional elements required. If you then fail to prove robbery on one of these elements, say that D is unlikely to be convicted of robbery, but that a theft conviction would be possible.

Check your understanding: 2 Application practice

2 Look back at 'Theft' at the beginning of this chapter to remind yourself of all the parts to the *actus reus* and *mens rea*. Apply these and the extra robbery elements to *Clouden*.

Answers on page 122

Summary

Actus reus:
- ✔ steals
- ✔ uses force or puts someone in fear of force
- ✔ immediately before or at the time.

Mens rea:
- ✔ dishonesty (MR for theft)
- ✔ intent to permanently deprive (MR for theft)
- ✔ **s 2** defences for theft may apply (MR for theft)
- ✔ plus an intention or recklessness to use force or the threat of it (MR for robbery).

Exam practice

Remember there are no essay questions in Unit 4A and the problem questions cover several offences so appear at the end of Chapter 11 (page 82).

Striving for an A/A*?

Learn the section numbers and subsections for each of the elements of theft carefully, noting any exceptions and with a case on each. This will enable you to relate the law accurately to the given facts and will provide a disciplined and logical approach to your application. This also applies to robbery because you need to prove theft before considering whether the addition of force (or the threat of it) may turn the theft into a robbery.

7 Burglary

Introduction

Burglary is different from theft and robbery in that it requires that D enters a building (or part of one) as a trespasser. There are two ways to commit burglary under **s 9 (1)** of the Theft Act 1968. There are common elements to these but important differences which you need to be clear on.

The two types of burglary
Revised

Under **s 9 (1) (a)** a person is guilty of burglary if:
- 'he enters any building or part of a building as a trespasser with intent to commit ...'
- an 'offence of stealing, inflicting grievous bodily harm, or doing unlawful damage'
- The emphasis here is on *mens rea*.
- D need not commit any of the specified offences (called ulterior offences)
- but must intend to do so when entering.

Under **s 9 (1) (b)** a person is guilty of burglary if:
- 'having entered any building or part of a building as a trespasser he steals or attempts to steal anything in the building or that part of it or inflicts or attempts to inflict on any person therein any grievous bodily harm'
- The emphasis here is on *actus reus*.
- D must either commit or attempt one of the two ulterior offences
- but need not intend to when entering.

The *actus reus* is mostly the same for both **(a)** and **(b)**; the *actus reus* and *mens rea* concerning the ulterior offences is where the difference lies.

Actus reus
Revised

The common *actus reus* elements are:
- enters
- any building or part of a building
- as a trespasser.

Entry
- In *Collins (1972)*, the CA said there must be an 'effective and substantial entry'.
- In *Brown (1985)*, leaning through a window was held sufficient, even though not substantial.
- In *Ryan (1996)*, entry was established, even though it was hardly effective.

Any building or part of a building

- 'Building' includes the obvious, like houses, offices and shops.
- It extends to vehicles or vessels that are inhabited (such as caravans and houseboats).
- Also to outbuildings and sheds.
- Whether more temporary structures are buildings is not always clear (see the key cases in the 'Now test yourself' box below).
- 'Part of a building' means that even if D has permission to be in some of the building, entering another part of a building can be enough for burglary.
- In *Walkington (1979)*, the customer had permission to be in the shop, but not behind the counter.

As a trespasser

In *Collins*, D had climbed the ladder to a girl's windowsill (naked except for his socks!) and she asked him in, thinking it was her boyfriend. Not only was the entry not 'substantial', but he had also been invited in so he didn't enter as a trespasser.

Smith and Jones (1976) shows that D may have permission but still be a trespasser by doing something in excess of that permission (taking the televisions).

Example

Susan is invited to a party. She has an argument with the host and is told to go. On her way out, she steals a coat. She can't be convicted of burglary under either subsection because she did not enter as a trespasser. Now consider the difference if she had been told to go and then gone into a bedroom and stolen some jewellery. Now she has entered part of a building (the bedroom) as a trespasser (she no longer has permission to be there) and can be charged with burglary.

Exam tip

Questions usually cover more than one offence so look carefully at the given facts. Look at the timing of the *mens rea*, especially if criminal damage occurs. This comes into **(a)** but not **(b)**, so if D causes criminal damage but there is no *mens rea* at the time of entry it will not be burglary, although it will still be criminal damage so you would discuss this (see Chapter 10 pages 72–74). Note the overlap with theft too. In the example on the left, you would discuss burglary and conclude Susan could not be convicted. She could be charged with theft of the coat so you would go on to explain and apply the law on theft.

Now test yourself

Tested ☐

1   Add the key cases to the brief facts and principle – the first two are done for you as these are not covered above.

B & S Leathley (1979)	A freezer container which had been in the same place for some time and was likely to remain there was found to be a building.
Norfolk Constabulary v Seekings and Gould (1986)	A trailer with electricity and shutters used as a temporary store was not found to be a building.
	A conviction for burglary was upheld when D went behind the counter in a shop and opened the till.
	The windowsill was not 'substantial' entry and D may not have been a trespasser as he was invited in.
	Leaning through a shop window to reach goods inside was effective entry. The CA said the word 'substantial' was unnecessary.
	Although a boy had a right to be in his father's house, this did not extend to stealing the television, as he had gone beyond any permission given.

Answers on page 122

Mens rea

Revised ☐

There are two parts to the *mens rea*, one regarding the trespass (which is the same for both subsections) and the second regarding the ulterior offence (which is different for each).

MR for the trespass

- D must know, or be reckless as to, the fact that there is no permission to enter the building, or that part of it.
- This was stated in *Collins*.
- It applies to both **s 9 (1) (a)** and **(b)**.

MR for the ulterior offence

- For **s 9 (1) (a)** the *mens rea* is intent to steal, inflict grievous bodily harm, or do unlawful damage:
  - MR must be present **at the time of entry as a trespasser**.
  - There is no further *actus reus* needed, however.
  - So D need not actually commit one of the ulterior offences.
- For **s 9 (1) (b)** the *mens rea* is that for the ulterior offences:
  - MR must be present **at the time of committing that offence**.
  - So for **(b)** D must steal or inflict GBH, or attempt to do so.
  - This means both *actus reus* and *mens rea* for the ulterior offence are needed.
  - Unlike for **(a)**, D needn't have intended to do so when entering.
  - However, for **(b)**, the ulterior offence must actually be committed.

Check your understanding: 1 Application practice

1 Martin is asked by a householder to fit a kitchen. While working in the house he asks to go to the toilet. Once upstairs he passes the bedroom door which is open and goes in. He sees some jewellery and takes it. Apply the law to decide if he has committed burglary and if so which subsection it would come under. Will it make a difference if he doesn't actually take the jewellery?

Answers on pages 122–23

Summary

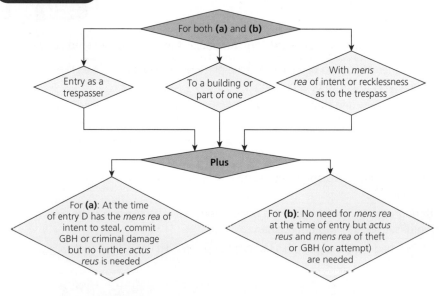

Exam practice

Remember there are no essay questions in Unit 4A and the problem questions cover several offences so appear at the end of Chapter 11 (page 82).

8 Blackmail

Introduction

Although blackmail also comes under the Theft Act there is no need for a theft to take place.

Under **s 21** of the Theft Act 1968 a person is guilty of blackmail:

'if, with a view to gain for himself or another or with intent to cause loss to another, he makes any unwarranted demand with menaces.'

The *actus reus* is:

- a demand
- the demand is unwarranted
- the demand is made with menaces.

The *mens rea* is:

- with a view to gain for himself or another, or
- with intent to cause loss to another.

Actus reus Revised ☐

The demand

- The demand can be by words, conduct or writing.
- Once the demand is made, this part of the *actus reus* is satisfied.
- V need not hear or receive the demand.

> **Case example**
>
> In *Treacy v DPP (1971)*, D wrote and posted a letter in England addressed to a woman in Germany. He demanded that she send £175 to him in England under the threat that if she did not he would send her husband photos of her with another man. The issue was whether he could be tried in England, but in deciding that he could, the HL made the point that if a demand is contained in a letter then that demand is made as soon as the letter is posted.

The demand is unwarranted

Under **s 21 (1)** a demand is unwarranted unless the person making it does so in the belief:

'(a) that he has reasonable grounds for making the demand; and

(b) that the use of the menaces is a proper means of reinforcing the demand'.

- It is a subjective matter.
- It is not what a reasonable person may believe but whether D believes the grounds are reasonable and the use of menaces is proper.
- The jury need to be satisfied that D believes **both** these things.

Case example

In *Harvey, Ulyett and Plummer (1981)*, the Ds had paid a man £20,000 for what was supposed to be cannabis but wasn't. Angry at being swindled, they kidnapped his wife and child and threatened to harm them if the money was not returned. The CA confirmed that **s 21 (1)** was concerned with the belief of the individual D in the particular case, and what a reasonable person may believe was irrelevant. However, it was also held that even if D believed there were reasonable grounds for the demand (which was accepted), no act which D believed to be unlawful could ever be believed to be proper.

The demand is made with menaces

- In *Harry (1974)*, during a student rag week, shopkeepers were offered immunity from 'inconvenience' in return for donations to charity.
  - This was held not to be sufficient 'menace' because the shopkeepers were unconcerned.

- In *Garwood (1987)*, D had threatened a rather timid person into giving him £10, but the threat was unlikely to have caused a normal person to react.
  - The CA held this would not usually be sufficient 'menace' but it could be if D was aware of the likely effect on the victim.

- In *Clear (1968)*, it was said to be 'with menaces' if a normal person would be affected by the threat.
  - It is not necessary to show that the *actual* victim was affected.

So, it is what D does and knows that matters, not the effect on the victim.

Case example

In *Strachan and McGuigan (2008)*, two men had tried to sell tapes containing allegations of a minor royal being involved in sex and drugs to various newspapers. When they failed to sell the story, they demanded £50,000 from the royal instead. However, he did not pay but contacted the police. Even though the royal had not paid the money demanded, the jury at the Old Bailey took less than five hours to reach a guilty verdict.

Now test yourself

Tested ☐

1 What are the three parts to the *actus reus* of blackmail?
2 What section of which Act is the offence found in?
3 What point was made in *Treacy*?
4 Why was the demand not found to be blackmail in *Harry*?

Answers on page 123

Exam tip

You often need to discuss more than one offence. Watch for the overlap between other Theft Act offences and blackmail, and with the defence of duress. Taking something from someone will be theft. If force is used it may be robbery but blackmail could be an alternative if there is a demand, e.g. for a payment to return the property.

Example

- I hit you and take your car. This is robbery because I hit you in order to steal.
- I then demand payment for its return. This may also be blackmail.
- I take your car from outside your house and demand payment for its return. This is not robbery (no force in 'order to steal'). It may be blackmail and will also be theft if there is an intention permanently to deprive.

Typical mistake

A common mistake is not to read the question carefully enough and to focus on only one offence. There is usually more than one alternative, so look at the overlap between the offences as you revise them.

Check your understanding: 1 Application practice

1 In *Raphael (2008)*, D took the victim's car by hitting him with a metal bar and then demanded payment for it to be returned. Apply the law in this unit so far to see what offences D could be charged with.

Answers on page 123

Mens rea

There are two alternative parts to the *mens rea*:

- a view to gain for oneself or another, or
- an intent to cause loss to someone else.

S 34 (2) (a) provides that 'gain' and 'loss' are to be understood as 'extending only to gain or loss in money or other property, but as extending to any such gain or loss whether temporary or permanent'.

- The intended gain or loss must be of money or other property.
- The gain or loss can be temporary.
- This is a *mens rea* issue so no gain or loss need actually be made (as seen in *Strachan*).
- There need only be intent in regard to a gain **or** a loss, not both, though often both will occur.
- 'Gain' includes a gain by keeping what one has – **s 34 (2) (a) (i)**.
- 'Loss' includes a loss by not getting what one might get – **s 34 (2) (a) (ii)**.

Now test yourself

5 Write down the definition of blackmail and pick out each part of the *actus reus* and *mens rea*. Then try to find a case or a section of the statute that adds to each of these elements.

Answers on page 123

Check your understanding: 2 Application practice

2 In *Bevans (1987)*, D was in severe pain and pointed a gun at a doctor, demanding that he inject him with morphine, a painkiller. Apply the law on blackmail to decide if he was guilty.

Answers on page 123

Exam tip

As well as considering other offences, as mentioned above, watch also for a possible defence of duress. A demand by Jim that John must rob a shop and hand over the proceeds would be blackmail by Jim, but could also be theft, burglary or robbery by John with a possible defence of duress. Be very careful to read the question to ensure whose liability you are asked to discuss.

Summary

D is guilty of blackmail under **s 21 (1)** if, 'with a view to gain for himself or another or with intent to cause loss to another, he makes any unwarranted demand with menaces'.

Actus reus	
Demand	The demand is complete once made, it does not have to be communicated – *Treacy v DPP (1971)*.
Unwarranted	Under **s 21 (1)** a demand is unwarranted unless the person making it does so in the belief **(a)** he has reasonable grounds for making the demand and **(b)** the use of the menaces is a proper means of reinforcing the demand.
	The demand is unwarranted where D knew the threatened act was unlawful – *Harvey (1981)*.
With menaces	A normal person would be affected – *Clear (1968)*.
	If D knows the particular victim would be affected even though a normal person might not be – *Garwood (1987)*.

There is an overlap between 'unwarranted' and 'with menaces' in that the greater the threat, or 'menace', the less likely the jury will be satisfied D believed it to be proper.

Mens rea	
With a view to gain for himself or another or	'Gain' includes a gain by keeping what one has – **s 34 (2) (a) (i)**.
With intent to cause loss to another	'Loss' includes a loss by not getting what one might get – **s 34 (2) (a) (ii)**.

Exam practice

Remember there are no essay questions in Unit 4A and the problem questions cover several offences so appear at the end of Chapter 11 (page 82).

9 Fraud and making off without payment

Introduction

The two offences of fraud which you need to know under the Fraud Act 2006 are:

- fraud by false representation – **s 1** and **s 2**
- obtaining services dishonestly – **s 11**.

This Act reformed the law on various deception offences but some older cases will still be used where the provisions of the Act are similar.

The other offence in this chapter is making off without payment, which comes under **s 3** of the Theft Act 1978.

Fraud by false representation s 2 (1)   Revised ☐

S 1 creates a single offence of fraud which can be committed in three ways. You only need fraud by false representation which comes under **s 2 (1)**. This offence is committed when D:

'(a) **dishonestly makes a false representation, and**

(b) **intends, by making the representation:**
    (i) **to make a gain for himself or another, or**
    (ii) **to cause loss to another or to expose another to a risk of loss.'**

The *actus reus* is:

- making a representation
- which is false.

Making a representation

- Under **s 2 (3)** a representation can be:
  - as to fact
  - as to law
  - as to state of mind.
- The representation can be express or implied – **s 2 (4)**.
- The representation can be made to a person or to a machine – **s 2 (5)**.

Examples

Representation as to fact	Using a false identity.
	Making an untrue statement about something you are selling.
Representation as to law	An untrue statement about how the law covers the transaction.
Representation as to state of mind	Saying you will pay a bill when you don't intend to.
Express representation	These can be written, spoken, posted on a website or communicated by conduct, e.g. over-quoting for work, giving a false reference, producing a false ID card.
Implied representation	Implying you are collecting for charity by wearing a false badge, implying you are someone else by wearing a particular uniform or giving a credit card without authority to use it.
Representation to a person or to a machine	Any of the above representations may be made to a person but **s 2 (5)** expressly covers representations made to 'any system or device', e.g. using a false card or coin in a machine or phishing on the internet.

Which is false s 2 (2)

A representation is false where:

'(a) it is untrue or misleading, and

(b) the person making it knows that it is, or might be, untrue or misleading'.

- Under **(a)** it has to be untrue or misleading.
- The effect on the person to whom it is made is irrelevant; the statement need not be believed.
- **(b)** is essentially part of the *mens rea*.

Key cases

Case	Brief facts	Type of representation
Silverman (1987)	An excessive quotation for work was given to elderly women.	Express – written or spoken: an untrue representation as to the actual cost.
Barnard (1837)	Wearing a university cap and gown and saying he was a member of the university to gain credit in a shop.	Express – spoken: the statement that he was a member. Implied – by conduct: implying he was a member by wearing the cap and gown.
Lambie (1981)	Using a credit card in Mothercare after the bank had withdrawn her authority to do so.	Implied – by conduct: implying she had authority to use the card by presenting it to the shop.
MPC v Charles (1976)	Using a cheque guarantee card and writing cheques for more than the amount agreed with the bank.	Implied – by conduct: implying he had authority to use the card for that amount.
Davies (2008)	D preyed on elderly people, asking for deposits for building work which was never done, or asking for money for investments which were never made.	Express – written and spoken: an untrue representation that the work would be done or the investments made.

The *mens rea* is:

- dishonesty
- intent to make a gain or cause a loss
- also for the representation to be false D must know it is, or might be, untrue or misleading.

Dishonesty s 2 (1) (a)

The guidelines to the Act make clear that the *Ghosh* test applies.

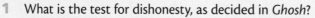

Now test yourself

Tested ☐

1. What is the test for dishonesty, as decided in *Ghosh*?
2. What type of representation was seen in *Barnard*?
3. If you use a credit card, what are you implying?
4. When might this be fraud?

Answers on page 123

Intent to make a gain or cause a loss s 2 (1) (b)

The law is very similar to blackmail on *mens rea*:

- It is a *mens rea* issue so no gain or loss need actually be made.
- The intended gain or loss must be of money or other property (property is as for theft).
- The intended gain or loss can be temporary.
- There need only be intent in regard to a gain **or** a loss, not both, though often both will occur.

Exam practice answers and quick quizzes at **www.therevisionbutton.co.uk/myrevisionnotes**

- 'Gain' includes a gain by keeping what one has.
- 'Loss' includes a loss by not getting what one might get.

D must know it is, or might be, untrue or misleading s 2 (2) (b)

This was seen opposite under 'which is false' but **s 2 (2) (b)** is part of *mens rea* and is a subjective test.

- D must know the representation is untrue or misleading.
- If it is untrue or misleading (AR) and D knows this (MR) then it is false.
- So it is a mix of *actus reus* and *mens rea*.

> **Examples**
>
> An IT programmer working for Sainsbury's stole loyalty scheme points from Nectar and redeemed £8,120 of the points for grocery shopping. This is similar to a person dishonestly using a credit card to pay for items. He falsely represented that he had a right to use the points in exchange for the groceries and he knew this was not true. He was convicted of fraud by false representation in 2011.
>
> Another modern problem that will be caught by **s 2** is 'phishing'. This is when someone pretends to be a bank or other business (a dishonest representation) and sends out bulk emails with the intent to 'catch' some of the recipients (intending to make a gain or cause a loss). This is done by directing them to what appears to be a genuine website which asks them to register details such as bank account or credit card numbers. With this information, the sender intends to gain access to the person's bank account or purchase goods using that person's identity (again intending to make a gain or cause a loss). D also knows that the website is false (so knows the representation is untrue).

Check your understanding: 1

During parliamentary questions in 2007, the government confirmed the following would be fraud by false representation. Apply these to an electrician offering to rewire a house, where he is paid in the first two situations but not in the third.

1 A bailiff repeatedly charges for work that has not been done.
2 A person represents himself to be a certificated bailiff, but is not, and by doing so obtains a payment or goods from a debtor.
3 A person represents himself to be a certificated bailiff, but is not, and intends by so doing to obtain a payment or goods from a debtor.

Answers on page 123

Obtaining services dishonestly   Revised ☐

Under **s 11 (1)** an offence is committed if a person 'obtains services for himself or another:

- **(a)** by a dishonest act, and
- **(b)** in breach of subsection **(2)**'.

Under **s 11 (2)** a person obtains services 'in breach of subsection 2' if:

- **(a)** they are made available on the basis that payment has been, is being or will be made for or in respect of them
- **(b)** they are obtained without any payment having been made for or in respect of them or without payment having been made in full and
- **(c)** when they are obtained the person
  - knows they are being made available on the basis described in **(a)**, or

– that they might be, but
– intends that payment will not be made, or not made in full.

John finds a gap in the fence and uses it to gain entry to a pop concert. He has obtained services – watching the concert. Climbing through the fence is a dishonest act and he knows that watching the concert is something that should be paid for and he intends not to pay. He has both *actus reus* and *mens rea* for the offence under **s 11** Fraud Act 2006.

Actus reus

The *actus reus* is:

- obtaining services by a dishonest act **s 11 (1)**
  - Unlike **s 2** above, a service must actually be obtained for the *actus reus* to be complete.
  - Also a dishonest act is required, again unlike **s 2**, the offence cannot be committed by an omission.
- on the basis that payment will be made **s 11 (2) (a)**
  - This includes any services where a fee is payable at some point.
- without such payment being made either in full or in part **s 11 (2) (b)**.
  - D does not pay the full price for the services obtained.

Mens rea

The *mens rea* is:

- dishonesty (a dishonest act is required under **s 11 (1) (a)** so again there is a mix of AR and MR here)
- knowing the services are, or might be, made available on the basis that payment will be made at some point (past, present or future) **s 11 (2) (c)**
- intending that payment will not be made, or will not be made in full **s 11 (2) (c)**.

Examples

- Obtaining internet or subscription satellite TV services (dishonestly using false details to obtain internet downloads or get TV channels cheaper, or for free).
- Obtaining cheap or free entertainment (watching a football match or concert without paying the full price).

Exam tip

There is an overlap between these two Fraud Act offences so you may need to discuss both. Using a fake ID to obtain a service of some kind could come under **s 11** (intending to gain by a service by falsely representing the right to use the ID) or under **s 2** (obtaining the services dishonestly). Note carefully that **s 11** requires the obtaining of the service actually to occur. This differs from **s 2** where there is no need to actually make a gain or cause a loss, just to intend to do so. Look for clues as to whether something has been gained or lost. This may help you decide the most appropriate charge.

Summary

S 1	Creates a single offence of fraud	*Actus reus*	*Mens rea*	Examples
S 2	**By false representation** There is no need actually to make a gain or cause a loss, just to intend to do so.	Making a false representation.	Dishonesty and intent.	• Charging for work not done. • Using false chip-and-pin details. • Phishing.
S 11	**Is a separate offence of**	*Actus reus*	*Mens rea*	Examples
	Obtaining services dishonestly This **does** require the obtaining of the service actually to occur.	Obtaining services on the basis that payment will be made without such payment being made either in full or in part.	Dishonesty, knowledge and intent.	• Climbing a fence to watch a football match. • Using a stolen credit card. • Using a decoder dishonestly.

Making off without payment

S 3 of the Theft Act 1978 provides that a person commits this offence where:

> 'knowing that payment on the spot for any goods supplied or service done is required or expected from him, dishonestly makes off without having paid as required or expected and with intent to avoid payment of the amount due.'

There are three parts to the *actus reus* and three to the *mens rea*:

- makes off – AR
- without having paid as required or expected – AR
- for goods or services supplied – AR
- knowing payment on the spot is required – MR
- dishonesty – MR
- intent to avoid payment – MR.

An example would be leaving without paying for petrol or a meal.

Makes off

- This essentially means 'depart'.
- There is no need to run away.
- However, D must leave the scene, so was not liable in *McDavitt (1981)* for refusing to pay a restaurant bill because he waited in the restaurant until the police came, so had not 'made off'.

Without having paid as required or expected

- Payment cannot be required or expected if what is supplied is illegal, e.g. drugs or stolen goods.
- Nor where the payment is not legally enforceable because it isn't yet due.
- In *Troughton v MPC (1987)*, D was drunk and asked a taxi driver to take him home. He couldn't remember exactly where he lived and they had an argument. The taxi driver took him to a police station where he ran off. Payment was not required or expected because the service was not complete (he was not driven home) so he was not guilty.

For goods or services supplied

- The supply of goods or services must have been completed.
- As seen above in *Troughton*, where he had made off without paying, but the service was not completed as the driver had not taken him home.

Knowing payment on the spot is required

- This is part of the *mens rea* (knowing) but has an element of *actus reus* (payment on the spot is required or expected).
- If payment on the spot is not required then D cannot 'know' that it is.
- In *Vincent (2001)*, it had been agreed that payment for hotel bills could be delayed. So D did not 'know' payment on the spot was required or expected.
- Even though it was expected at some point it was not expected 'on the spot', so he was not guilty.

You get a taxi back from the office Christmas party. You haven't any money so can't pay when the driver asks for the fare. You thought the taxi journey was on the firm's account and a bill would be sent to you later. Alternatively, you believed that your employer was paying for transport home for all staff. In neither case do you 'know payment is required on the spot'. You have not committed an offence.

Dishonesty

- The *Ghosh* rules will be applied.
  - Was D's act dishonest by the ordinary standards of reasonable and honest people?
  - Did D realise the act would be regarded as dishonest by such people?
- Note, however, that D won't be dishonest if there was a genuine reason for not paying.

I order a meal in a restaurant. When it eventually arrives, I eat a few mouthfuls but it is cold and inedible so I refuse to pay for it and leave. I have made off, and payment on the spot was required, and I know this. However, as I have a genuine reason not to pay, I have not been dishonest so the *mens rea* is not fulfilled.

Intention to avoid payment

- It must be shown that D had no intention of *ever* paying; a temporary intention is not enough.
- In *Allen (1985)*, D left his hotel without paying the bill and said he intended to pay later.
- The HL held D must intend to avoid paying permanently and this was a question for the jury. His conviction was quashed.

Now test yourself

Tested ☐

5 Add the principle to the column on the right.

Case	Brief facts	Principle
McDavitt (1981)	D refused to pay for his meal but stayed in the restaurant until the police came.	
Troughton (1987)	D was drunk and asked a taxi driver to take him home. They had an argument and he ran off before getting home.	
Vincent (2001)	It had been agreed that payment for hotel bills could be delayed.	
Allen (1985)	D left his hotel without paying the bill but said he intended to pay later.	

Answers on page 124

Exam tip

This offence also has some common elements with the two offences under the Fraud Act, including dishonesty and obtaining services. Look carefully at the facts to see which offences may be appropriate, especially noting whether all parts of the *actus reus* and *mens rea* are satisfied. The 'Check your understanding: 2' box opposite should help with this.

Check your understanding: 2 Application practice

4   In *DPP v Ray (1973)*, D and some friends ordered a meal in a restaurant and after the meal, they decided to leave without paying. They waited until the waiter left the room and then ran out. Apply the law in this chapter to show whether a charge for any of the three offences could succeed.

Answers on page 124

Summary

S3 Theft Act 1978	*Actus reus*	*Mens rea*
Making off without payment	Makes off – *McDavitt* Without paying as required or expected – *Troughton* For goods or services supplied – *Troughton*	Knowledge that payment on the spot is required – *Vincent* Dishonesty – *Ghosh* Intent to avoid payment permanently – *Allen*

Striving for an A/A*?

These offences overlap. You need to concentrate on being clear about the similarities and differences between them so you can apply the law confidently. Do some research on the cases so that you really understand the principles and the way they apply in different circumstances.

Exam practice

Remember there are no essay questions in Unit 4A and the problem questions cover several offences so appear at the end of Chapter 11 (page 82).

10 Criminal damage

Introduction

There are three separate offences under the Criminal Damage Act 1971 **s 1**:

- criminal damage **s 1 (1)** – the basic offence
- criminal damage with intent to endanger life **s 1 (2)** – the aggravated offence
- arson **s 1 (3)** – criminal damage by fire.

The last can also be with intent to endanger life but there is no separate section for this. It would be both **s 1 (2)** and **s 1 (3)**.

Criminal damage s 1 (1)   Revised ☐

S 1 (1) provides:

> 'A person who without lawful excuse destroys or damages any property belonging to another intending to destroy or damage any such property or being reckless as to whether any such property would be destroyed or damaged shall be guilty of an offence'.

There are four parts to the *actus reus*:

- destroys or damages
- property
- belonging to another
- without lawful excuse.

Destroys or damages

To destroy property would be to make it useless but damage is much wider. A few examples will best illustrate this.

Key cases

Case	Brief facts	Whether it was criminal damage and why
Hardman v CC of Avon & Somerset Constabulary (1986)	Protesters used water-soluble paints on pavements.	Yes, the council were put to the expense of cleaning the pavements.
R v A (a minor) (1978)	D spat on a policeman's overcoat.	No, the spittle could be easily removed with a damp cloth.
Roe v Kingerlee (1986)	D smeared mud on the walls of a police cell.	Yes, even though not permanent it cost money to clean.
Morphitis v Salmon (1990)	D caused scratches on scaffolding.	No, it did not impair the usefulness or value of the property.
Fiak (2005)	D blocked the toilet in his prison cell with a blanket causing flooding.	Yes, the blanket and three cells had to be cleaned.

Exam practice answers and quick quizzes at **www.therevisionbutton.co.uk/myrevisionnotes**

We can identify several principles which arise from these cases:

- It is likely to be criminal damage if someone is put to the expense of repairing or cleaning.
- It is not likely to be criminal damage if there is no impairment to usefulness or value.
- What may be criminal damage in one case may not be in another:
  - A scratch on scaffolding is different from a scratch on a painting or a car, for example.

Property

The definition of property for the offence of criminal damage is similar to that for theft, but there are slight differences.

- Mushrooms, flowers, fruit or foliage of a plant growing wild on any land are not property, unlike theft.
- You cannot damage intangible property, so this is also excluded.
- You can damage land so this is included.
- Wild creatures which have been tamed or are ordinarily kept in captivity are property, as with theft.

Belonging to another

Again, this is similar to theft.

- It includes another having custody or control of property, having a right in property or having a charge on it.
- However, it is not criminal damage if you destroy or damage your own property.
- Nor if you destroy or damage property which you honestly believe is yours.

In *Smith (1974)*, a tenant caused damage to other fixtures when removing wiring which he had installed with the landlord's permission. In law, all fixtures had become the landlord's property, so belonged to another. However, the CA quashed the conviction because he believed the property was his so he had a right to damage it (see also under *mens rea* over the page).

Without lawful excuse

Under **s 5 (2)** there are two lawful excuses to causing damage, so there is no offence if D believes that:

- **(a)** the person with rights in the property would consent to the damage, or
- **(b)** the property was at risk and in immediate need of protection, and what was done was reasonable in the circumstances.
- D's belief must be honestly held but need not be reasonable.
- Although part of the *actus reus*, these 'excuses' are essentially defences to causing damage.

Again, a few cases will help to explain how they work in practice.

Key cases

Case	Brief facts	What the court held
Jaggard v Dickenson (1981)	D was drunk and broke into a house thinking it was her friend's and believing the friend would have consented to the damage caused.	Her belief only had to be honest; her drunkenness did not invalidate this so she had a lawful excuse under **s 5 (2) (a)**.
DPP v Blake (1993)	A vicar used a marker pen to write a biblical quotation on a wall outside parliament in protest about the Gulf War. He claimed he had God's consent.	Nothing within the meaning of the Act covered consent by God so he did not have a lawful excuse under **s 5 (2) (a)**.
DPP v Blake (1993)	The vicar also argued that property in the Gulf needed immediate protection.	The property was too far away, so incapable of being protected by his actions so he did not have a lawful excuse under **s 5 (2) (b)**.
Chamberlain v Lindon (1998)	D demolished a neighbour's wall which blocked his right of access to his own property. He had an honest belief that his property rights needed immediate protection.	The means adopted were reasonable, having regard to all the circumstances so he had a lawful excuse under **s 5 (2) (b)**.
Cresswell and Currie (2006)	Ds destroyed traps which had been set for badgers and argued that they were protecting property (the badgers).	**S 5** only applies to protecting 'property' 'belonging to another'. The badgers were not property (because they had not been tamed or kept in captivity) and did not belong to another (no one yet had custody or control of them) so the Ds could not rely on **s 5** at all.

Examples

- Many cases have resulted from protesters damaging GM crops:
  – to protect other crops.
- Other cases have involved protesters damaging, or writing slogans on, walls and fences around nuclear installations:
  – to protect potential damage to property in the area, and beyond.
- The arguments of protecting property have rarely succeeded.
- Either because the property did not need 'immediate' protection or because the actions were not 'reasonable in the circumstances'.

Exam tip

Criminal damage may well come up with a question on theft or one of the related offences. Look out for things like 'D broke into the house to steal something'. Burglary will be the obvious crime, but a discussion of criminal damage in relation to the breaking in can earn extra marks. Unless, that is, the question specifically asks you to discuss only offences under the Theft Act. As always, read the question carefully.

Mens rea

- Intention to destroy or damage property belonging to another, or
- recklessness as to whether such property is destroyed or damaged.

Case example

In *Gemmell and Richards*, two boys aged eleven and thirteen set light to some papers outside the back of a shop and several premises were damaged. The HL decided recklessness should be subjective, not whether the risk of damage was obvious to a reasonable person but whether they themselves saw a risk of damage. Thus, their ages should be taken into account and as they were young and would not have realised the risk of the fire spreading, the HL overturned their conviction.

- The intention or recklessness must relate to 'property' 'belonging to another'.
- An honest belief that D owns the property negates the *mens rea* (as in *Smith*).

Example

I break up some of my old furniture to put on the fire because I have run out of firewood. I intended to destroy it, but am not guilty of criminal damage because the furniture did not 'belong to another'. If it turns out one of the chairs I broke belonged to my lodger then whether I am guilty will depend on whether I honestly believed it was mine. If I did not realise it was not one of mine then I am still not guilty of an offence.

Destroying or damaging property with intent to endanger life s 1 (2)

Revised

This is often referred to as 'aggravated' criminal damage. Under **s 1 (2)**:

> 'a person who without lawful excuse destroys or damages any property, whether belonging to himself or another:
>
> (a) intending to destroy or damage any property or being reckless as to whether any property would be destroyed or damaged; and
>
> (b) intending by the destruction or damage to endanger the life of another or being reckless to whether the life of another would be thereby endangered;
>
> shall be guilty of an offence'.

- This is similar to criminal damage but with the addition in **(b)** that D intended or was reckless with regard to endangering life. It is a much more serious offence with a maximum sentence of life imprisonment.
- A difference is that the damage does not have to be to property belonging to another.
- Destroying your own property will suffice if there is intent or recklessness as to endangering life.
- The 'lawful excuse' defence does not apply; this can only be used for the basic offence.

Intending by the destruction or damage to endanger life

- Note the word 'by'; this indicates there is an issue of causation.
- The danger to life must be caused by the damage.

In *Steer (1987)*, D shot at the house of a former business partner, causing damage. This did not extend to the aggravated offence because any danger to life came not from the damage but from his action of firing the shots.

- If D intends to endanger life that is enough.
- It is purely a matter of *mens rea*.
- There does not necessarily have to be a danger to life.

Example

I cut the brake cable on someone's bike because I have a grudge against the owner. I know that life will be endangered as soon as it is ridden. As it happens, the owner has just got a new bike. The old one is taken apart for spares and never ridden. I have not actually endangered life – but I intended to do so. I am guilty of aggravated criminal damage because I have damaged property (AR), I intended to damage property (MR) and I also intended to endanger life by that damage (MR).

Check your understanding

1 In *Sangha (1988)*, D set fire to some furniture in an empty flat belonging to his neighbour. The flats were designed so that other flats would not be affected by a fire. Briefly explain the *actus reus* and *mens rea* of the aggravated offence and apply it to these facts to see if all elements of AR and MR are satisfied.

Answers on page 124

S 1 (3) provides:

'An offence committed under this section by destroying or damaging property by fire shall be charged as arson'.

- This is also regarded as a serious offence with a maximum sentence of life imprisonment.
- There must be criminal damage as above under **s 1 (1)** or **s 1 (2)**.
- If the damage was caused by fire it will be arson.
- So there can be arson contrary to **s 1 (1)** and **s 1 (3)** – the basic arson offence – or
- arson contrary to **s 1 (2)** and **s 1 (3)** – the aggravated arson offence.

Case example

In *MPC v Caldwell (1982)*, D set fire to a chair in the hotel where he worked. Although the fire was put out before anyone was harmed he had endangered the lives of the residents. He was convicted of arson contrary to **s 1 (2)** and **s 1 (3)**. This case was overruled by *Gemmell and Richards* on the issue of recklessness. Now it would be a question of whether he knew there was a risk of endangering life, not whether a reasonable person would see the risk. This would depend on whether he knew there were people in the hotel that could be in danger from the fire. If not, it would be arson contrary to **s 1 (1)** and **s 1 (3)**.

- Arson can be committed by omission if there is a duty to act.

Now test yourself　　　Tested

1　What were the facts of *Miller* (see Chapter 1 page 9)?
2　What was the omission?
3　What type of duty did he owe?
4　Which criminal damage offence would apply to these facts?
5　Why was he found guilty?

Answers on page 124

The lawful excuse defence can be used for arson too:

- In *Denton (1982)*, D set fire to his employer's mill and successfully argued that his employer had consented to this in order to make a fraudulent insurance claim.
- The lawful excuse defence can only be used for the basic offence.
- If the damage by fire is done with intent to endanger life then lawful excuse cannot be used.

Summary

The offence	Criminal damage – the basic offence	Criminal damage – the aggravated offence	Criminal damage by fire – arson	Case example
Section number	s 1 (1)	s 1 (2)	s 1 (3)	
Actus reus	Damaging or destroying property belonging to another	Damaging or destroying property need not belong to another	Damaging or destroying property by fire belonging to another **s 1 (1)** or not **s 1 (2)**	*Hardman (1986)* *Roe (1986)* *Smith (1974)*
Mens rea	Intent or subjective recklessness as to whether property is damaged or destroyed	As for **s 1 (1) and** as to endangering life	As for **s 1 (1) and/or** as to endangering life **s 1 (2)**	*Gemmell and Richards (2003)*
Defence	Lawful excuse plus general defences	General defences only	Lawful excuse only if with **s 1 (1)** plus general defences	*Blake (1993)*

Exam practice

Remember there are no essay questions in Unit 4A and the problem questions cover several offences so appear at the end of Chapter 11 (page 82).

11 Defences

Introduction

The defences you need for Unit 4A are intoxication, self-defence and the prevention of crime and duress, together with duress of circumstances. Intoxication, self-defence and the prevention of crime were covered in Unit 3A, so see Chapter 5 (pages 36–48) for these. This chapter will cover duress and duress of circumstances.

- Duress is where there is a threat of harm if D does not commit a particular crime.
- If there is a direct threat from another person it is known as duress by threats.
- If the threat comes from the surrounding circumstances, rather than from another person, it is called duress of circumstances.
- Some of the law relates to both.
- Both can be used for all crimes except murder or attempted murder.

> **Typical mistake**
>
> Some students jump straight to defences without first discussing the offence because they have immediately spotted something in the scenario that indicates a particular defence. Unless an offence has occurred, there is no need for a defence, so this is bad practice.

Duress   Revised ☐

- The threat has to be of death or serious harm, *Valderrama-Vega (1985)* (the death threat could support the defence but not the threat to disclose his homosexuality).
- The threat can be to D or D's family, or someone for whom D is responsible such as a car passenger, as in *Conway (1988)*.
- The rules on duress were laid down in *Graham (1982)*.

The test for the jury set out in *Graham*

There is a two-part question for the jury:

1 Was the defendant compelled to act because there was good cause to fear serious injury or death?

2 If so, would a sober person of reasonable firmness, sharing the characteristics of the accused, have responded in that way?

- The first may seem to be a subjective question, but in *Hasan (2005)*, it was held, obiter, that the belief must be reasonable.
- That it is an objective question was implied in *Graham*, which refers to D having 'good cause to fear'.
- The second question is objective, what a reasonable person would do.
- However, the reasonable person shares D's characteristics.
- The characteristics which can be shared are those which would affect D's ability to resist.

- In *Bowen (1996)*, his low IQ was not taken into account, as it didn't affect his ability to resist the threat. However, the CA accepted the following characteristics would be relevant to the second question:
  - age
  - sex
  - pregnancy
  - a serious physical disability
  - a recognised mental illness or psychiatric disorder.
- These could make D more susceptible to a threat and/or lower the ability to resist threats.
- Note the words 'sober person'. In *Graham*, D had been drunk as well as threatened but the court said that voluntary intoxication could not be taken into account.

Is there a safe avenue of escape?

- If there is an alternative option the defence will fail as in *Gill (1963)*, where D stole a lorry under threat but had several opportunities when he was alone to raise the alarm.
- The threat need not be immediate, as long as it was still influencing D at the time of the offence.
- In *Hudson and Taylor (1971)*, two young girls lied in court because they were told they would be harmed if they testified against the accused.
  - The judge ruled that as the threat wasn't immediate the defence could not be used.
  - The CA allowed their appeal and held that it was irrelevant that the threat could not be carried out immediately, as long as it was having an effect on D at the time of the offence (and they were still frightened).
- Similarly, in *Abdul-Hussain (1999)*, the CA held that duress did not need an immediate threat, as long as it was influencing D at the time of the offence.

The threat must be to commit a specific offence

- Mostly the defence applies where someone says 'commit this offence or else', but it is a little more than this.
- A couple of examples will best explain it.

Case examples

In *Cole (1994)*, a man had been threatened because he owed money. He then committed robbery in order to pay off the debt. He said he only did this because he was in fear for his life and that of his girlfriend and child. The defence of duress was rejected because he had not been under a threat to commit robbery.

In *Wadsworth (2010)*, a woman was charged with theft. She admitted stealing but said she did it under duress from her former boyfriend. They had been in a relationship since she was sixteen and she said she lived in fear of violence from him and believed he would kill her or her family if she did not bring cash home for him. The defence of duress succeeded as she specifically stole to give him money and she had good reason to fear serious harm.

Self-induced duress

If D voluntarily associates with people who are violent, the defence will not succeed if violence is then used.

Key cases

Case	Brief facts	Whether the defence is available
Sharp (1987)	D joined a gang known to be violent. They threatened him when he wanted to withdraw from committing a robbery.	The CA rejected the defence of duress as he knew they might use violence and threaten him, so the threat was self-induced.
Shepherd (1987)	D joined a gang not known to be violent. They threatened him when he wanted to withdraw from shoplifting.	His defence succeeded as both the gang and the activity was non-violent so the threat was not seen as self-induced.
Hasan (2005)	D associated with a drug dealer known to be violent. The dealer threatened his family to make D commit burglary.	The defence failed because he voluntarily associated with criminals and 'ought to have foreseen' the risk of being threatened.

The rules as stated in *Hasan*

The rules on duress were restated and clarified by the HL in *Hasan*.

- The threat relied on must be to cause death or serious injury.
- The criminal conduct which it is sought to excuse has been directly caused by the threats.
- The threat must be directed to D or a member of D's family, or to 'a person for whose safety the defendant would reasonably regard himself as responsible'.
- D may rely on duress only if there was no evasive action that could reasonably have been taken:
  - such as going to the police, disapproving *Hudson and Taylor*.
- The questions for the jury were both objective:
  - did D 'reasonably believe' there was a threat, approving *Graham*?
- The defence is not available where, as a result of a voluntary association with criminals:
  - D 'ought reasonably to have foreseen' the risk of violence.
  - This is a little stronger than *Sharp*, which required that D 'knew' they were violent.

Duress of circumstances

Revised

- This is where D acts under duress not because of a specific threat from a person, but from threatening circumstances.
- Duress of circumstances was established in the mid-1980s.
- Most early cases involved some kind of driving offence to avoid a threat. The following are three examples:

Exam tip

If there is no evidence in the given scenario of a threat from a person, look for any circumstances that may be threatening, and consider duress of circumstances. There still needs to be a threat of physical harm, whichever defence is used; it is where the harm comes from that differentiates the two.

Key cases

Case	Threatening circumstances and offence	Principle
Willer (1986)	A gang of youths surrounding the car appeared threatening (reckless driving).	There is no need for a specific threat as long as D acted under a compulsion, or duress.
Conway (1988)	D's passenger told him to drive off quickly as there was a threat from two men running towards the car (reckless driving).	There need not be a threat (they were actually policemen) as long as D reasonably believes there is.
Martin (1989)	The threat came from his wife threatening to commit suicide if he didn't drive his son to work (driving while disqualified).	The *Graham* test applies to duress of circumstance.

Exam practice answers and quick quizzes at **www.therevisionbutton.co.uk/myrevisionnotes**

The defence was extended beyond driving cases in *Pommell* (1990), where D was convicted of possessing an offensive weapon. He said he had taken it to stop the person who had it from hurting someone, and as he did not want to carry it around at night he planned to take it to the police the next morning. The CA held duress of circumstances applied to all crimes except murder and attempted murder and ordered a retrial.

Now test yourself

Tested ☐

1 What is the *Graham* test, as approved in *Hasan*?
2 Briefly explain how the test applies using a different case.
3 Can duress of circumstances apply where the threat is to another person?
4 Give a case example for your previous answer.
5 Which threat in *Valderrama-Vega* could support a defence of duress and which could not?

Answers on page 124

Typical mistake

It is a common mistake to misread the question and discuss the wrong person; usually this means covering blackmail instead of duress. Read the question carefully and make sure you only discuss the liability of the person you are asked about.

Example

Ahmed threatens to beat up Yoko's family if she does not steal from her employer and give him the money. The exam question asks you to discuss Yoko's liability. This means you should explain and apply the law on theft then discuss the possibility of defence of duress (apply the rules on this). No marks at all are gained by discussing any liability of Ahmed for blackmail, even if that is a real possibility, as you were not asked for this.

Case example

In *Hasan* (2005), D associated with a drug dealer who was known to be violent. The dealer threatened that if D didn't burgle a house to steal money from a safe there, he and his family would be harmed. He was charged with burglary and argued that he acted under duress. The HL restated the law on 'voluntary associations' and confirmed that the defence was not available where D foresaw, or ought reasonably to have foreseen, the risk of being subjected to any compulsion by threats of violence. The HL added that if the harm threatened was not immediate, or at least imminent, then D should take evasive action, e.g. by going to the police. The HL judgement included a summary of the essential requirements for duress as discussed above.

Check your understanding: Case example

1 Referring to the case example of *Hasan* above, complete the left-hand column with the six points which were made or confirmed by the HL, then match as many of these as you can to earlier cases on the same points of law. The first is done for you as an example.

Requirements of the defence of duress as stated by the HL in *Hasan*	Earlier case on the same point
The threat relied on must be to cause death or serious injury.	*Valderrama-Vega* (1985)

Answers on pages 124–25

Summary

Don't forget to revise Chapter 5 (pages 36–48) on intoxication and self-defence. The summary includes these:

Defence	Main points	Which crimes	Effect
Intoxication – involuntary	Must remove *mens rea* – *Kingston (1994)*.	All crimes requiring *mens rea*.	Acquittal.
Intoxication – voluntary	Only applies to specific intent crimes and must remove *mens rea* of intent – *Majewski (1976)*.	Specific intent crimes. Basic intent crimes.	Reduces to basic intent crime. Guilty because D is reckless in getting drunk.
Self-defence	Force must be reasonable. Any mistaken belief that self-defence is needed must be genuine but need not be reasonable.	All.	Acquittal.
Duress	Direct threat of imminent death or serious injury to force D to commit a crime.	Not murder or attempted murder.	Acquittal.
Duress of circumstances	Threat of imminent death or serious injury by circumstances.	Not murder or attempted murder.	Acquittal.

Exam practice

AQA June 2012

Dan found a council car-parking permit, valid for a further 28 days, on the pavement. Though he intended to hand the permit in to the council offices, he first displayed it in his car for several days to obtain free parking, which should have cost £70. After the permit had expired, Dan did indeed hand it in at the council offices. The following day, Dan ordered a meal in Gwen's café. When he started to eat, he was so disgusted with the quality of the meal that he changed his mind about paying, and left without doing so.

Gwen engaged Ben, an electrician, to repair the electrical wiring in the downstairs living room of her house. Ben owed £1000 to Reggie, a violent man. Reggie knew that Ben was working at Gwen's house. Reggie told Ben that there would be 'big trouble' for him and his family unless he stole money from Gwen in order to reduce the debt. The following day, while Ben was working in Gwen's living room, she left the house to go shopping. Ben immediately remembered Reggie's threat and went upstairs to see whether there was anything worth stealing. While searching Gwen's bedroom, he found, and decided to keep, £50 and a black rubbish bag containing some old, but expensive-looking, clothes which Gwen had decided to throw out. When Gwen suddenly returned and confronted Ben in the bedroom, he pushed her over as he ran out with the money and the rubbish bag. Gwen fell heavily against a wardrobe and broke her arm.

1 Discuss Dan's possible criminal liability for property offences arising out of his obtaining and using the parking permit and his failure to pay for the meal. **[25 marks]**

2 Discuss Ben's possible criminal liability for property offences arising out of his activities in Gwen's house. **[25 marks]**

Answers online

Online

Unit 4 Section C: Concepts of Law

Introduction

This unit is divided into five chapters covering five different concepts of law:

- law and morals
- law and justice
- judicial creativity
- fault
- balancing conflicting interests.

This unit is synoptic, which means it connects to the other law you have studied, not just the substantive law (crime, contract or tort), but the institutions and procedures you studied for AS. You will be expected to show your understanding of these by relating them to the more theoretical concepts found here, for example, how far the law involves issues of morality or how far it achieves justice. For judicial creativity, you will have a good base to build on because you have studied precedent and statutory interpretation. Here you need to consider how and whether these allow judges to be creative and make law. Fault is a major element of criminal law but, as you will have seen when studying for AS, there are some crimes of strict liability where no fault has to be proved. In tort, there are also some areas of strict liability although most torts require at least negligence. For conflicting interests you need to look at how the law can be used to engineer a balance between the competing interests of the parties concerned and also the public interest.

You can use any cases you know to illustrate these concepts. Where possible I have used examples from the other units so they will be familiar to you, but I have added some more contemporary cases which may be new to you. You should try to include some modern examples to show you understand the importance of these five concepts of law in today's society.

The examination

- Examinations take place once a year in June. (The last January exams were in 2013.)
- The exam lasts 2 hours but this includes Unit 4A which should take 1 hour.
- You are advised by AQA to spend 15 minutes preparing your answer.
- There are three essay questions.
- You must answer one question from these.
- Each question is worth 30 marks (15 marks each for AO1 and AO2) plus an additional 5 marks for quality of written communication (AO3).

Help from the exam board

- The AQA website has a lot of important and useful information and guidance. It tells you what you need to cover in each topic and explains the Assessment Objectives (AO1, AO2 and AO3).

- There are plenty of past examination papers, together with mark schemes and examiners' reports.

- It is important to look at these for revision because they give you helpful guidance on what should be covered in order to reach the higher grades.

Preparing for the exam

- You need to be prepared to answer questions on all the topics in the unit. The material in this Revision Guide will help you do this, but you should also look at previous papers, mark schemes and reports to prepare properly for the exam.

- To gain high marks, answers need to be relevant to the question asked. It is important to be selective and not just to write down all you know about an area. This approach does not gain marks because it indicates that you do not know how to apply the *relevant* law.

- The level of detail needed will depend on how many areas of law are covered. Where there are several areas to be covered, less detail will be expected.

- You should revise the material thoroughly, so that you go into the exam with confidence.

- You need to understand the law, not just to be able to reproduce it. You will need to adapt it to answer questions that are slightly different from those that you may have answered before.

- You should practise answering questions under exam conditions so you can learn to manage your time efficiently.

Use of authorities

- You will need to refer to authorities in support of your answer; these include examples, cases and Acts of Parliament.

- For cases, the date of the case is not important and with long or complicated case names it is sufficient to use a shortened version. Examiners will know which case you mean. Criminal cases are usually written *R v*, but in most law textbooks (including this Revision Guide) the cases are referred to by the name of the defendant only.

- For Acts of Parliament, it is important to include the date and to know the different section numbers for the different parts of the *actus reus* and *mens rea*.

12 Law and morals

Introduction

Law and morals is about whether the law is, or should be, based on moral values or whether they are separate issues. You will need to be able to explain the nature of moral and legal rules, how each come about and the differences between them. You will need to show your understanding of the substantive law, by relating this to the more theoretical concepts found here, with examples.

What is 'morality'? Revised

- Morality is based on what people believe to be acceptable.
- Different societies make rules to govern people's behaviour.
- Rules can arise over time through customs or beliefs.
- Rules may be enforced by the community or family or church.
- There is no shared morality; there are divergent views on what is acceptable behaviour, depending on factors such as culture and religion.
- Adultery, abortion and gay marriage are examples.
  - In some countries these are crimes.
  - In England some people may see them as morally wrong, but they are not illegal.

Case example

In *Gillick v West Norfolk and Wisbech AHA (1986)*, a mother brought a case arguing a doctor had no right to prescribe contraceptives to her daughter.
- The case went all the way to the HL, and even there it was only a 3–2 majority decision, showing there was disagreement between the judges right up to the highest level.
- The HL held that children under sixteen had the right to make their own decisions on treatment as long as they were competent to do so.

What is law? Revised

There is no easy answer and judges, lawyers and academics disagree over how to define law, however there are a few general statements that can be made about law.

- Law is made by Parliament or the courts.
- Sometimes moral rules may become law through the courts or through Parliament; then the rules can be enforced by the courts and legal penalties can be imposed for breaking the rules (see examples).
- There are certain characteristics of law that don't apply to morality (see table on page 86).

These are moral issues but some have now become legal issues too:
- fox hunting
- smoking in public
- lying
- drinking alcohol in the street
- cheating in exams
- abortion.

The basic differences between law and morals

Revised

Characteristics of moral rules	Characteristics of legal rules
They develop slowly over a period.	They can be made overnight.
They are voluntary.	They are not voluntary.
They *ought* to be obeyed.	They *must* be obeyed.
There is no official sanction for breaking the rules.	Breaking legal rules results in official sanctions.
They are enforced by the disapproval of society.	They are enforced through the courts.

- There is a significant overlap between morality and law. Crimes such as murder, robbery and rape are usually seen as both immoral and illegal.
- When discussing law and morals the main thing to consider is whether the rules governing behaviour should be illegal, and so enforceable in court, or purely a matter of individual moral values governed by society alone.
- There are differing theories on this:
  - A supporter of natural law sees law and morals as interlinked.
  - A positivist sees the two as separate, and a matter for the individual.

Natural law

Revised

- Natural law is based on morality.
- A supporter of natural law sees law as coming from a higher source – God or nature.
- An immoral law need not necessarily be obeyed.

Positivism

Revised

- A positivist looks more scientifically at the law.
- If a law has been correctly made it should normally be obeyed, even if it is immoral.

In 1957, the **Wolfenden Committee** recommended that prostitution and homosexuality in private should no longer be criminal. This led to a major debate about law and morals.

- Professor Hart (a positivist and an academic) agreed with the Committee.
- Lord Devlin (a supporter of natural law and a judge) disagreed.

Hart's view

- Law and morality should be separate.
- Morality is a private matter.
- The law should not be used to enforce morality.
- The state should not intervene to restrict the freedom of the individual, unless the conduct could harm others.

Devlin's view

- Law and morality were inseparable.
- The law should intervene to support morality.
- Immoral acts could undermine society.
- Judges should enforce moral rules to protect society, as was seen in *Shaw v DPP (1961)*.

Hart was influenced by the philosopher John Stuart Mill, who believed that the law should allow people the freedom to make their own choices, so long as they do not harm others.

Check your understanding: 1

1 In *Airedale NHS Trust v Bland*, the HL held the doctors could remove the feeding tubes which were keeping the patient alive. Add a comment both for and against the decision, if possible referring to one of the theories in support. This will help you produce a balanced argument.

Answers on page 125

One problem with morality being enforced in court is that opinion changes, as with homosexuality and prostitution. In addition, advances in medical technology make new things possible, as with stem cell research on embryos and manipulation of genes to produce 'designer babies'. If there is no shared opinion on whether something is morally right, it is arguable that the law should leave matters to individual choice.

Case example

Quintavalle v Human Fertilisation and Embryology Authority 2005

A couple had been granted the right by the Authority to use 'tissue typing' to select an embryo that would be a match for their son who needed a transplant. This would mean an embryo that was not a match would be discarded. Mrs Quintavalle, from the pressure group CORE (Comment on Reprographic Ethics), challenged this, saying it could lead to people having embryos tested for other characteristics, such as sex or hair colour ('designer babies'). The HL ruled that selection was allowed under the Human Fertilisation and Embryology Act 1990.

Following this case, the government issued a consultation paper to assess public opinion. The Human Fertilisation and Embryology Act 2008 was passed after this consultation. Tissue typing can be licensed where a sibling suffers from a serious medical condition. Sex selection on social grounds is generally prohibited, but allowed if serious harm could otherwise occur, e.g. through a gender-related hereditary disease. The case and the subsequent Act show how the law has to make moral decisions to keep up with medical advances.

Exam tip

There is much disagreement between the academics and judges who have written about these concepts and you are not expected to be absolute on the issue one way or the other. The main thing, when it comes to the examination, is to keep your answer and examples relevant to the specific question asked and, where possible, use one or two of the theorists to support what you say.

Now test yourself

1 State three differences between law and morals.
2 Did Hart believe law and morals to be separate or linked?
3 In what circumstances did Hart say that the law could be involved in a moral issue?
4 Would a natural law follower believe law and morals to be separate or linked?

Answers on page 125

Law and morals in relation to criminal law

- There are many criminal cases which have a moral element, especially where there is an act of violence.

Offences against the person

- *Brown* and *Wilson* are prime examples of criminal cases with a moral element (see Chapter 5 page 46).
- There is not usually a legal duty to act, though there may be a moral one.
- However, in *Stone and Dobinson* there was not just a moral duty, but a legal one – as also in *Gibbins and Proctor* (see Chapter 1 page 9).
- In *R v R (1991)*, the court held that a man could be convicted of raping his wife. Society's views had changed and the law had to keep up.
- Many defences have a moral element too:
  - Some defences recognise that although legally wrong, there may be a reason or excuse for an act.
  - Loss of control and diminished responsibility cases can be used to show that even murder can be partially excused, and sometimes a mandatory life sentence may be morally wrong.
  - The defences of insanity and automatism also show an element of morality as they apply where D does not recognise the act is wrong or is not in control.
  - Intoxication is rarely allowed as a defence as it would be morally wrong for D to use being drunk as an excuse to commit a crime.

Offences against the property

- Theft, robbery and burglary provide examples:
  - It is illegal as well as immoral to steal, though arguably there are times when stealing is morally acceptable, e.g. to feed a starving child.
- If you receive property by mistake you have a legal, not just a moral, duty to return it – *A-G's Reference (No 1 of 1983)*.
- The *Ghosh* test asks the jury whether D is dishonest by ordinary standards. This may involve a moral assessment – what the jury believe is right or wrong.
- In criminal damage cases protesters are often acting for reasons they believe are morally just (e.g. against war, nuclear weapons, GM crops).
- Duress can be a defence where someone has been forced to commit a crime, so not morally at fault, but is not available if the charge is murder.

Check your understanding: 2

2 Look up the cases of *Pretty v DPP* and *Re B*, both in 2002. Can you see the difference in the facts that allowed the court to come to different decisions? Hint: the case of *Bland* might be useful.

3 Which 2009 case followed *Pretty*, and what happened in that case?

Answers on page 125

Law and morals in relation to civil law

- A moral link can be seen in *Donoghue v Stevenson (1932)*, where Lord Atkin developed the biblical idea of 'love thy neighbour' to 'do not harm your neighbour'.

- The *Donoghue* case is an example of how the courts may be prepared to develop the law of tort to protect the consumer, who is usually in a weaker position.

- The Consumer Protection Act followed and is an example of Parliament following the courts on changes to the law.

- In *White*, the police were unable to succeed in a claim for psychiatric harm, in part because it would be immoral to allow the police to get compensation but not the victims' families.

- In *BRB v Herrington (1972)*, the HL held BRB owed a 'common duty of humanity' to a child trespasser and later, Parliament reflected and enforced this morality by passing the Occupiers' Liability Act 1984.

- The Unfair Contract Terms Act and Unfair Terms in Consumer Contracts Regulations show that Parliament may also 'interfere' to protect the weaker party in consumer contracts, e.g. by limiting the ability of a business to exclude liability (**UCTA**) or impose unfair terms (**UTCCR**).

- Both Parliament and the courts offer protection to weaker parties by imposing terms in certain contracts, e.g. the Sale of Goods Act, the Supply of Goods and Services Act and *The Moorcock (1889)*.

Law and morals in relation to contemporary issues

As there is no 'shared morality', disputes often arise as to whether the law should allow/not allow a certain type of behaviour. There were many debates prior to relaxing the law on prostitution and homosexuality and, more recently, prior to the bans on smoking and fox hunting. Other issues where there is much disagreement are:

Euthanasia and assisted suicide

- This issue can be discussed along with murder and manslaughter cases.

- There is a fine line between assisted suicide and murder.

- Should an individual be able to make their own decisions about ending their life?

- Should anyone who helps them be prosecuted?

- Case example: *Pretty*.

'Designer babies'

- Should people be able to choose the genetic make-up of their babies?
- Should they only be able to do this for medical reasons?
- Should the individual be able to decide or should it be a matter of law?
- Case example: *Quintavalle v Human Fertilisation and Embryology Authority.*

Now test yourself

Tested

5 What is a 'shared morality' and why is not having this important in relation to moral issues?
6 Why is intoxication rarely allowed as a defence?
7 Give an example of a case where the law changed to keep up with changing social values, and in what way.
8 Give an example of a case where the law changed to keep up with medical advances, and in what way.

Answers on page 125

Check your understanding: 3

4 Look up the facts of *Brown* and *Wilson*. In both cases, the 'victim' consented, but the legal decisions conflicted. Why do you think the majority of the judges decided as they did in *Brown* but a different decision was reached in *Wilson*?

Answers on page 125

Summary

- ✔ Morality is based on what people believe to be acceptable.
- ✔ Different societies make rules to govern people's behaviour.
- ✔ Rules can arise over time.
- ✔ Rules may be enforced by the community or family or church.
- ✔ There is no shared morality; views differ on what is acceptable behaviour.
- ✔ Law is made by Parliament or the courts.
- ✔ Sometimes moral rules may become law through the courts or through Parliament, then they can be enforced by the courts and penalties can be imposed for breaking the rules.
- ✔ Natural law is based on morality:
  - A supporter of natural law (e.g. Devlin) sees law as coming from a higher source – God or nature.
  - An immoral law need not necessarily be obeyed.
- ✔ Positivism looks at the law scientifically:
  - A supporter of positivism (e.g. Hart or Mill) sees law as based on rules.
  - If a law has been correctly made it should normally be obeyed even if it is immoral.

Exam tip

Read the question carefully. You may be asked to show the relationship between law and morals or to explain how the law might promote or enforce legal values. There will not be a 'right answer' and you can form your own opinion to some extent, but be careful of voicing personal views too strongly, and make sure you support what you say.

Typical mistake

Students are often tempted to go too far into the rights and wrongs of an issue that they feel strongly about, e.g. fox hunting. An examiner does not want to read what you think about fox hunting, but to see how you can use such an example to support an argument that the law is needed (or not) to enforce morality.

Points for an essay

There are a huge number of issues that can be discussed in an essay, and many different approaches, so this is not a list of what you should include but an indication of what you need to be able to do to produce a basis for an essay. You should be able to:

● distinguish between law and morals and illustrate their similarities and differences

● recognise and illustrate the diversity of moral views

● identify the opposing academic and judicial views on the relationship between law and morals

● explain how the issue of law and morals relates to the substantive law (crime, tort and/or contract)

● illustrate the way in which the issue of law and morals is still of importance today in relation to cases such as those involving assisted suicide, 'designer babies', religious clothing or other current issues

● explain how the law may be used to promote or enforce morality, with cases and/or examples

● produce an argument for and/or against the law promoting/enforcing morality, using case examples.

Exam practice

AQA June 2011

Consider the view that there is a close relationship between law and morality. Examine the debate as to whether the law should reflect moral values, and discuss issues which show the continuing importance of that debate.

[30 marks + 5 marks for AO3]

Answers online

Online

13 Law and justice

Introduction

There are several theories on the meaning of justice and you will need to be able to discuss some of them. There is no 'right answer' to what justice means, so don't worry too much about whether you agree, but you will need to be able to explain some of the main arguments.

The meaning of justice Revised

So what is justice? A simple idea of justice is that of fairness and equality and it is, or should be, the primary aim of a legal system to deliver justice. However, although we may equate law with justice there are many occasions when the law fails to produce justice (otherwise we would not need appeal courts or the Criminal Cases Review Commission).

> **Exam tip**
>
> Don't try to learn everything about all the theories because you won't have time to discuss many of them in any detail. It is better to pick out the ones that make the most sense to you. Your essay will be more confident and it will be easier for you to use examples if you understand the arguments and points raised.

Theories of justice Revised

The table below contains a brief explanation of the main theories (see also the previous chapter).

The theories	Main points	Proponents of the theories
Natural law	Law comes from a higher source, God or nature, and is linked to morality. An immoral law should not normally be obeyed. To Aristotle, justice could be distributive (benefits and burdens are distributed fairly through society) or corrective (the law should correct any imbalance).	Aquinas and Aristotle
Positivism	A more scientific approach where law is based on rules and is separate from morality. For a positivist, a bad law would still be valid and should be obeyed. To Hart, justice could be procedural (people having access to justice, a fair system of courts and tribunals, the right to appeal, etc.) or substantive (the law itself is just and applies equally and fairly to everyone).	Hart and Kelsen
Utilitarianism	This looks at the consequences of a law, and asks whether it benefits more people than it harms. A law should maximise happiness and provide 'the greatest good for the greatest number'. Individual rights are unimportant in this theory, however Mill believed the state should not interfere with people's freedoms unless harm could be caused to others.	Bentham and Mill
Economic theories	Similar to Utilitarianism, however these theories look at measuring happiness in terms of material wealth. To Marx, wealth should be distributed fairly in society (not necessarily equally); to Nozick there should be no redistribution of wealth if it had been obtained in a just manner.	Marx, Rawls and Nozick

Does the law achieve justice?

Revised

There are two main questions when considering whether, or how far, the law achieves justice:

- Is the legal system just (procedural justice)?
- Is a particular law just (substantive justice)?

You can refer to any areas of the law you have studied, both on the legal process and on crime and contract or tort.

Now test yourself

Tested

1   Which theory of justice regards law as coming from a higher source?
2   State one argument in favour of the utilitarian approach to justice.
3   State one argument against this approach.
4   Which theory of justice is based on rules and ignores any moral content?

Answers on page 125

Here are a few points you could consider when discussing whether justice is achieved.

The legal system and justice

- Trial by jury (gives protection to D and balances inequality between the state and the individual).

- The appointment and independence of judges (to achieve a fair and unbiased trial).

- Access to justice and the financing of court cases (to balance inequality in financial means, but arguably there are still many restrictions and no real equality of access to the law).

- The appeals system and the Criminal Cases Review Commission (both of these correct injustices which may have occurred as in *Kennedy* – see Chapter 3 page 24 – but their very existence indicates that injustice occurs).

- Sentencing (taking account of mitigating and aggravating circumstances) may help achieve justice; but a deterrent sentence seeks to stop the behaviour reoccurring rather than attempting to achieve justice in the particular case (which may be unjust as regards the offender):
  - The mandatory life sentence for murder recognises the severity of the crime so seems just at first sight. However, it also means the judge cannot take any mitigating circumstances into account.

- Remedies can achieve justice by compensating C for any harm caused, but individual rights may give way to those of society, e.g. by the refusing of an injunction in *Miller v Jackson (1977)*:
  - Equitable remedies, such as injunctions and rescission, will only be granted if injustice won't be caused.

- Precedent (treating like cases alike is just in that it is based on equality; the other rules of precedent help to avoid any injustice caused by applying this rule too strictly).

Typical mistake

Many students correctly identify a law or procedure which seems unjust but fail to go further and connect this to any of the theories, merely noting that the law is unsatisfactory in some way, which will gain very few marks.

Exam tip

Avoid the typical mistake by referring to a law you think is unjust or wrong and going on to show you understand some of the theories by explaining why that law is in conflict with particular ideas of justice, such as fairness, equality or individual rights. You can say, for example, a law is unjust because people are denied natural justice by being treated unequally or unfairly. You could also say someone may be denied a remedy because their rights have given way to the utilitarian idea of achieving the maximum happiness for the most people. Always use cases or examples in support of what you say.

The substantive law and justice

- Strict liability crimes allow a criminal conviction without proof of *mens rea* which is arguably unfair.

- In *Brown*, (see Chapter 5 page 46) the possible effect on society of immoral behaviour outweighed the rights of the individuals to consent to harm.

- The removal of the need for loss of control to be sudden under the Coroners and Justice Act may improve justice for women, but as loss of control still needs to exist, women are arguably still at a disadvantage and not on equal terms with men in domestic violence cases.

- Contract terms may be implied by both statutes and the courts to protect weaker parties, especially in consumer contracts. This helps to correct any imbalance in the powers of those entering contracts.

- A duty of care is owed only where it is 'fair, just and reasonable' to impose one, so many tort cases involve a consideration of what is best for society – what will maximise happiness.

- The standard of care in tort is based on what a reasonable person would do, so individual characteristics are not taken into account – as with the learner driver in *Nettleship v Weston (1971)*. The individuals in such cases are treated equally but the result is arguably unfair.

- Vicarious liability makes an employer liable for the wrongs of an employee. This may give justice to the victim but the employer is not at fault so this can seem unfair.

- The Protection of Freedoms Act 2012 reduced the detention without charge of terrorist suspects to a maximum of fourteen days. Many people had protested that the idea of locking someone up without charge was against natural justice and was unfair.

Case examples

In *Gilderdale (2010)*, a woman killed her daughter in an assisted suicide and was found not guilty of murder and given a twelve-month conditional discharge. In *Inglis (2010)*, in similar circumstances, the mother was sentenced to life because she was found guilty of murder. These cases show the difficulty with having a mandatory life sentence. Once murder is established the judge has no discretion, so Mrs Inglis was given life even though it was accepted she acted in what she believed were her son's best interests. These two cases also show not only that people will disagree on what justice is, but also on whether it has been achieved. Many agreed with the decision in *Gilderdale* and thought the jury made the right decision and that justice was done, but many others thought that justice was not done because she had taken a life.

In *Rogers v Swindon NHS Primary Care Trust (2006)*, a woman took her local Health Trust to court for not supplying a new drug, Herceptin, shown to reduce the risk of recurrence of breast cancer. It cost £20,000 per year. The CA held that the refusal even to consider her for treatment was illegal. This is a difficult question of justice. If treatment is expensive and funds have to be allocated from limited resources, this will reduce what is available for other patients. The utilitarian approach to justice would most likely favour a more balanced approach so that more patients could be treated (although it should be remembered that it is total happiness that is measured, so one person being very happy and many people not being happy would still meet the utilitarian concept of justice). In 2008, the National Institute for Clinical Excellence (NICE) published a report which said that if drugs are too expensive the NHS should not have to provide them, even if they would prolong life. This may mean Health Care Trusts have a stronger argument against prescribing expensive drugs. The CA's point in *Rogers* was not that all treatment should be funded, but that the policy in relation to funding should be fairer and more transparent, i.e. more just.

Exam practice answers and quick quizzes at **www.therevisionbutton.co.uk/myrevisionnotes**

Re A (2000)

Jodie and Mary were born joined at the spine. Mary's heart and lungs did not function and her blood supply was provided by Jodie. Without an operation to separate them, it was very likely that both twins would die. However, the operation would mean that Mary would definitely die because she would no longer have the blood supply from Jodie. Their parents opposed surgery because they believed it was wrong for one child to die to save the other; this would be against natural law. The CA held that the doctors would have a defence to any possible charges based on the fact that it was necessary to operate to save Jodie and so they went ahead with the operation. Mary would have died with or without the operation, but Jodie would have a good chance of a long and healthy life only if it was performed.

There were very strong views about whether justice was achieved in this case, and Ward LJ said, 'Everyone seems to have a view of the proper outcome. I am very well aware of the inevitability that our answer will be applauded by some but that as many will be offended by it'.

Those opposed to the operation regarded life as sacrosanct and believed the law should not intervene to allow the operation. Those in favour regarded the fact that Jodie would have a good chance of a full life as being paramount, and as Mary would die anyway, it was better to perform the operation.

Check your understanding

Refer back to case example *Re A (2000)* above, then answer the following questions.

1. How do you think a utilitarian would decide this case?
2. The parents did not feel they received justice; what do you think?
3. Can you find support for your answer in one of the theories of justice?
4. Do you think the law should be involved in such issues?
5. Where there is conflict between parents and doctors, who do you believe should make the final decision?

Answers on pages 125–26

Typical mistake

There is a clear overlap between justice and morals (the three cases are examples of this) and students often fail to focus on the correct area. A law which is immoral may well be unjust, but concentrating on the immorality of it will not gain you marks. You need to highlight the relevant theories of justice with which such a law would be in conflict.

Exam tip

When using an example which has a moral element to it you could explain one or more of the theories of justice and how these relate to your example. Then explain that under the natural law theory of justice an immoral law need not be obeyed, but that to a positivist, as long as the law was validly made with the correct procedures in place, then it should be obeyed regardless of its morality. Add a couple of examples and you will earn your marks because the focus of your answer will be on law and justice rather than law and morals.

Now test yourself

Tested

5   Add the proponents of the theories of justice to the right-hand column.

Natural law	This theory says law comes from a higher source – nature or God – and a just law must be moral.	
Positivism	This theory says law is based on clear rules and is separate from morality.	
Utilitarianism	This theory says a just law is one which maximises happiness.	
Economic theories	These theories attempt to measure happiness in economic terms.	
Substantive justice	This is whether a particular law is just.	
Procedural justice	This is whether the legal system and institutions achieve justice.	
Distributive justice	This is where benefits and burdens are distributed fairly through society.	
Corrective justice	This is how the law can correct injustice.	

Answers on page 126

Summary

Once you have completed 'Now test yourself' question 5 on the previous page, check your answers on page 126 then use the completed table as the chapter summary.

Points for an essay

As with law and morals, there are many different approaches to an essay question, so this is not a list of what you should include; it is a guide to what you need to be able to do to produce a basis for an essay. You will need to pick out from the question the particular issues that you need to focus on because, although there is a similarity between questions, there is usually a different emphasis. You may be asked to discuss the extent to which the law is successful in achieving justice, to explore the relationship between law and justice, and/or to discuss the difficulties involved in trying to achieve justice. You should therefore be able to:

● explain some of the different theories as to the meaning of justice

● explain how the issue of justice relates to the substantive law of crime, tort and/or contract (substantive justice)

● explain and evaluate the role of justice in the legal system (procedural justice)

● explain and evaluate how the law may correct injustice or address an imbalance (corrective justice)

● explain and evaluate how far the law achieves, or fails to achieve, justice

● explain and evaluate the difficulties the law has in achieving justice

● illustrate your evaluation by reference to cases and examples

● use cases where the parties involved disagree, or where society is divided on the issue, as these will be useful when discussing the difficulties the law has in achieving justice for all

● refer to the points listed on pages 93 and 94 when discussing how and whether justice is achieved and any difficulties which may arise.

Striving for an A/A*?

Go to the library and see if you can find other texts on the subject of justice. Different people have different ideas, as you can see from the theories, so a wider range of reading may help your understanding and provide you with other examples. If you don't have time for that, look at the news. There are often cases or proposals for new laws that produce protests. If people are protesting against a law or legal decision, it is often because there is an issue of justice involved, with one group regarding the case or law as unjust and another group in favour of it, as with the case examples on the previous pages.

Exam practice

AQA June 2011

Discuss the meaning of justice. Critically analyse the extent to which the law is successful in achieving justice, and discuss the difficulties which it faces in seeking to do so.

[30 marks + 5 marks for AO3]

Answers online

Online

14 Judicial creativity

Introduction

This area is based on your knowledge of judicial precedent and statutory interpretation from Unit 1. Although Parliament is seen as the supreme law maker, there are ways in which laws can also be created through judicial decisions. There are two ways this can happen: through the use of the rules of precedent and through statutory interpretation.

Exam tip

Although you will need to refer to what you learnt in Unit 1, you should bear in mind that at this level you will be asked to explain this in relation to a particular aspect of creativity, e.g. how far it is true to say that judges make law and/or whether or not it is a good thing for them to do so. Read the question carefully and, rather than stating everything you know about precedent and/or interpretation, *use* this knowledge to support and illustrate your answer to the specific point raised.

Do judges make law?

Revised ☐

This is arguable. It seems from many decisions that judges are making new laws or filling in the gaps in old laws. When a new situation arises, a judge may have to be creative because there is not yet a law which covers it, as with new technology and medical advances. However, not everyone accepts that judges make law.

- Some say judges make law and that this is a good thing.
  - Professor Hart (see Chapter 12 pages 85–91) was of this opinion and said that as rules are indeterminate and have an 'open texture', judges must 'fill in the gaps'.
  - Lord Denning was a judge who agreed with Hart that judges needed to fill any gaps in the law. He was in favour of creativity by judges.
- Others say judges do not make law, but only apply existing principles to new facts.
  - An academic who was strongly opposed to Hart, Ronald Dworkin, thought this.

Case example

Donoghue v Stevenson can be used for both arguments:
- It can be said a new law was made and this was good because it gave protection to consumers; there was a 'gap' in the law because previously only people with a contract had protection.
- It can be said that the principle of not harming others already existed in the law and that this principle was applied to a new situation, for a manufacturer of goods to have a duty not to negligently harm a consumer.

Whichever argument you prefer, both the rules of precedent and statutory interpretation can be used by judges to make changes in previous laws.

Now test yourself

1 Why might a judge need to be creative?
2 Why does Hart say judges must 'fill in the gaps'?
3 Who else said judges must fill in the gaps?
4 Who argues that judges are merely applying existing principles and not making law?

Answers on page 126

Creativity and the rules of precedent

Here is a quick reminder of the main rules:

- **Following**
    - The basic rule is *stare decisis*, or let the decision stand.
    - Courts must follow earlier decisions of higher courts and usually themselves; they should treat like cases alike.

- **Distinguishing**
    - An earlier decision can be avoided by any court where the material facts are different.

- **Overruling**
    - Earlier decisions can be overruled by a higher court.
    - The Supreme Court (previously the House of Lords) can overrule its own earlier decisions using the **1966 Practice Statement** if 'it appears right to do so'.
    - The rules from *Young (1944)* allow the CA to overrule its own earlier decisions in particular circumstances.
    - The criminal division of the CA can also avoid following a precedent where it is dealing with the 'liberty of the subject' and it is necessary to do so in the interests of justice.

From this, it can be seen that there is some flexibility to the rules and these allow for creativity.

How can precedent allow creativity?

- **Following**
    - Although this seems to offer no choice, there is still a chance of creativity.
    - The *ratio decidendi* can be difficult to find, especially if the judgement is complex.
    - In the appellate courts, decisions are based on a majority, so there are several judgements from which to find the *ratio*.
    - In either case, it is the later judge who decides what the *ratio* is, thus allowing for an element of creativity.

- Case example: the 'neighbour principle' in *Donoghue v Stevenson* was seen by many as *obiter dicta* but was followed in several later cases as the *ratio decidendi*.

- **Distinguishing**
  - Although this can only be done where the material facts are different, which facts are material may depend on the judge's view.
  - It applies to any court so allows for quite a lot of creativity.
  - Case example: in *Wilson*, the CA did not follow the HL decision in *Brown* and ruled that consent could be a defence to serious harm. What the judge saw as different in the material facts was not the amount of harm, but that it occurred between a married couple and was for a 'bodily adornment'.
- **Overruling**
  - The **Practice Statement** allows the Supreme Court (previously the HL) to overrule its own earlier decisions.
  - This gives a wide discretion and allows an old law to be changed and a new one created.
  - Case example: in *Gemmell and Richards*, the decision in *Caldwell* was overruled by the HL and a new law created that made all recklessness subjective.
  - However, not many cases get to the SC and also the use of the **Practice Statement** has been kept to a minimum for the sake of consistency.
  - Case example: A criminal example is *Clegg (1995)*, where the HL criticised the law on how much force could be used in self-defence, but refused to change it.
  - Case example: A civil example is *Transco v Stockport BC (2004)*, where the HL recognised the problems with the tort under *Rylands v Fletcher (1868)* but made clear it was for Parliament, not the courts, to make any further changes.
  - The **Young** rules allow the CA to overrule its own earlier decisions in certain circumstances, but these are limited so only allow a little creativity.

Typical mistake

Students often correctly explain the rules but do not make clear to which courts they apply. This means any discussion of how far a judge can be creative will not be fully clear.

Exam tip

Avoid the mistake by being clear on which rules apply to which courts. Although distinguishing applies to all courts and thus allows for flexibility, the higher the court, the greater the opportunity to be creative. Don't forget to use case examples to explain *how* the rules allow for creativity.

Now test yourself — Tested ☐

5 What is the basic rule of precedent?
6 To which court does the Practice Statement apply?
7 Which rule of precedent applies to any court?
8 In what circumstance can the CA criminal division overrule its own earlier decisions?

Answers on page 126

Creativity and the rules of statutory interpretation — Revised ☐

Here is a quick reminder of the main rules.

- **Literal rule** – follow the words of the Act mechanically and do not try to 'second-guess' what Parliament may have intended.
- **Golden rule** – if application of the literal rule would lead to an absurd result, interpret the Act so as to avoid the absurdity.
- **Mischief rule** – look at the previous law and then at what 'mischief' the new Act was intended to prevent and interpret it accordingly.
- **Purposive approach** – look at the whole purpose of the Act and what Parliament was trying to achieve when passing it.

Although called 'rules' these methods of interpretation are not applied in any consistent way as the judge can choose which rule, or approach, to take and different judges will choose different approaches. How far the rules allow for creativity will depend on which is chosen.

A final rule is that under **s 2** of the Human Rights Act 1998, judges must consider the European Convention on Human Rights when interpreting statutes:

- If a law is incompatible with the convention the judge can point this out, but cannot change it – this respects Parliament's supremacy.
- However, judges may interpret statutes widely in order to satisfy human rights.

How can statutory interpretation allow creativity?

- **Literal rule**
  - This does not allow for any creativity because the judge follows the words of the Act mechanically even if the result is not what was intended by Parliament.
  - Case example: In *Fisher v Bell (1961)* the words 'offer for sale' were interpreted in strict accordance with contract law, so that a flick-knife in a shop window was not technically an offer for sale. This meant the shop owner was not guilty of offering a weapon for sale.

- **Golden rule**
  - This allows very little creativity because it is only used where the application of the literal rule would lead to an absurdity.
  - Case example: This could have been used in *Fisher v Bell* to avoid the absurd result that the Act became ineffective in preventing the display of weapons for sale.

- **Mischief rule**
  - This allows for some creativity because the judge will decide what 'mischief' the Act was intended to prevent and interpret it accordingly.
  - Case example: In *Smith v Hughes (1960)*, the Act was intended to stop the 'mischief' of prostitutes soliciting in public and the judge interpreted the words 'in the street' as including places which could be seen from the street by the public. Therefore prostitutes on balconies or in windows could be guilty of soliciting in the street.
  - If this approach had been used in *Fisher v Bell* it could also have meant he was guilty as the 'mischief' the Act was trying to prevent was exactly this type of situation.

- **Purposive approach**
  - This looks at the purpose of the Act as a whole, and what Parliament was trying to achieve. Effectively, where the literal rule looks at the strict letter of the law, this approach looks instead at the spirit of the law.
  - Again, if this approach had been used in *Fisher v Bell* it could also have meant he was guilty as the purpose of the Act was to prevent this type of situation.
  - Case example: In *Jones v Tower Boot Co. (1997)*, a man suffered serious racial abuse from other employees. The CA decided that the purpose of provisions in the Race Relations Act, which made employers liable for the actions of employees 'in the course of employment', was to encourage employers to prevent abuse of

this kind. The CA therefore interpreted the words 'in the course of employment' widely enough to include such behaviour, so the employer was liable.

- Judges are now allowed to consult Hansard, which records the debates in Parliament during the passing of an Act, so this may help them to find what Parliament was trying to achieve.

Now test yourself

9   Does the literal rule allow any creativity?

10 What may help judges to know what Parliament's intention or purpose was, and why?

11 Which rule, or approach, was used in *Fisher v Bell*?

12 When can the golden rule be used?

Answers on page 126

Should judges be creative?

This is arguable either way; there are good and bad aspects to creativity:

- Use of the literal rule, as well as the strict rule of precedent, leaves it to Parliament to fill in any gaps in the existing Acts.
  - This seems right as Parliament is the supreme law maker and is elected.
  - However, politicians are sometimes reluctant to act, especially in controversial areas like murder and euthanasia.

- Use of the purposive approach is (supposedly) giving effect to Parliament's wishes, or purpose:
  - This is perhaps better in one way as the decision should reflect Parliament's intentions at the time of passing the Act.
  - However, the judge in the particular case will have to decide what those intentions were, which may not be accurate.
  - This is particularly true of an old Act, e.g. the Offences Against the Person Act 1861.

- Just using one case (*Fisher v Bell*) we can see that the rules may lead to different results.

- If different judges use different rules there will be inconsistency in the law and this is not a good thing:
  - This is also true of distinguishing where different judges may see different facts as material.

- The need for certainty and consistency supports following the letter of the law, using the strict rule of precedent and the literal rule where possible:
  - However, justice in a particular case may indicate a need to be creative.
  - Case example: In *Gemmell and Richards*, the boys did not recognise the risk of the fire spreading so it was not fair, or just, to ask what a reasonable adult would foresee and this objective test was abolished.

- Another argument against creativity is that judge-made law applies retrospectively, at least to the parties in court:
  - Case example: A criminal example is *R v R*, where at the time D acted his actions were not a crime because it was not possible to rape your wife, so he would not have been guilty under the existing law.
  - Case example: A civil example is *Donoghue v Stevenson*, where at the time the snail got into the ginger beer a manufacturer did not owe a duty to a consumer, so would not have been liable under the existing law.
  - Parliament makes law which only applies to the future, i.e. a certain behaviour is prohibited *from now on*.
- Another argument for creativity is that the law can keep up with changing times:
  - Case examples: Both *R v R* and *Donoghue v Stevenson* can be used to support an argument that creativity was good for the victims in each case because under the existing law neither the wife nor the consumer were protected.
  - Also, if Parliament does not approve of the judgement it can pass an Act to overrule it.

Check your understanding: 1

1 Give an argument both for and against each of the following, with an example:

   a) overruling

   b) the literal rule

   c) the purposive approach.

2 Give two arguments against judicial creativity in general.

3 Give two arguments in favour of judicial creativity in general.

Answers on page 126

Summary

Rule of precedent or interpretation	Whether or not it allows any judicial creativity
Following (*stare decisis*)	is not creative, but provides certainty in the law.
Distinguishing	can be quite creative, but much depends on the judge's interpretation of what is material. Distinguishing applies to any court, although a lower court may later be overruled if seen as too creative.
Overruling	is creative as a new law is made and the old overturned. However, the **Practice Statement** only applies to the Supreme Court and the rules in *Young* only apply to the CA.
Literal rule	is not creative; the judge follows the law to the letter.
Golden rule	goes a little further, but only if the literal rule leads to absurdity.
Mischief rule	can be quite creative, but the judge only looks at what Parliament is trying to remedy.
Purposive approach	is the most creative rule of interpretation. The judge follows the spirit rather than the letter of the law in looking at the whole purpose of the Act.
Also note the use of Hansard	to find what members of Parliament intended at the time the Act was made.

Points for an essay

As with all the concepts of law, there are many different ways to approach a question. You will need to pick out the particular issues that you are being asked to focus on, because although there is a similarity between questions there is usually a different emphasis. This means it is not possible to say what you must cover in all cases, but the following is a guide to what you need to be able to do:

● Explain the rules of precedent (following, distinguishing, overruling).

● Explain which rules apply to which courts.

● Explain the rules of statutory interpretation (literal, golden and mischief rules, purposive approach).

● Explain which rules allow for creativity (see the table opposite).

● Explain which rules restrict creativity (see the table opposite).

● Use cases and examples to illustrate your points.

● Read the question carefully to see whether you need to also address the issue of whether judges *should* make law.

Check your understanding: 2 Exam practice

4 Read the following opening paragraph, written in answer to part of an exam question which asks whether the rules of precedent allow judges to be creative. Explain why this would not gain marks and write a paragraph of your own to show how you could improve it. You may need to double the length, although the content is more important than the number of words.

'The main rule of precedent is *stare decisis* which means let the decision stand and follow the earlier decision. However, a judge can distinguish a previous decision and so not follow it if the facts of the case are different. Also a previous decision can be overruled by a higher court and the Supreme Court can use the Practice Statement to overrule its own decisions as it did in *Gemmell and Richards*. Most courts have to follow their own earlier decisions though, but the Court of Appeal can overrule itself in certain circumstances as set out in *Young*. The criminal CA can overrule its own earlier decisions if it is in the interests of justice to do so. These rules show that judges can be creative.'

Answers on pages 126–27

Striving for an A/A*?

Read some original judgements to see whether judges were reluctant to change the law or not. You won't want to read them in full as many are quite long, but if you scan through a few pages, you can pick up some excellent information about what the judges themselves felt about the law. Quotations from judges will enhance an essay and provide you with accurate support for your evaluation.

Example: In *Gemmell and Richards*, the judge in the case clearly thought the law was wrong but said to the jury, 'it is my task to expound the law to you as it is, and it is your duty to apply the law as it is – not as you might like it to be'. The issue of how to interpret the word 'malicious' and how to define recklessness went to the HL, which used the **Practice Statement** to change the law.

The case archive is at the following link and you can then search by date and name (this one was called *R v G and another (2003)* at the time). The above quotation is on the first page of the judgement: **www.publications.parliament.uk/pa/ld/ldjudgmt.htm**.

For Supreme Court cases since 2009, try the following link: **www.supremecourt.gov.uk/decided-cases/**.

15 Fault

Introduction

Fault generally implies a sense of blameworthiness, or responsibility for one's wrongdoing. The concept of fault is seen in both criminal and civil law, mainly in the different levels of *mens rea* for various crimes and the standard of care in negligence. Some areas of both criminal and civil law have liability without fault, so we will also look at strict liability in this chapter.

Criminal liability and fault　　　　　　　　　　　　　　　　Revised ☐

- Intention is the highest level of fault:
  - Intention is the *mens rea* for murder, **s 18 OAPA** and theft.
- For most crimes the level of fault is recklessness:
  - All recklessness is now subjective, Cunningham recklessness, as confirmed in *Gemmell and Richards* (see Chapter 1 page 10).
- Manslaughter can be committed by 'gross negligence'.
- Defences can reduce or even remove the fault element.

Defence	Effect of defence and level of fault
Diminished responsibility	Recognises D is not fully responsible due to an abnormality of mental functioning so there is a reduced level of fault, making D guilty of manslaughter, not murder.
Loss of control	Recognises D has lost control for a specified reason, so there is a reduced level of fault, making D guilty of manslaughter, not murder.
Automatism	This means D is not in control at all, so not at fault and acquitted.
Insanity	Recognises D is not fully responsible so there is a reduced level of fault and a special verdict, allowing the judge to choose which order is most appropriate.
Voluntary intoxication	This can negate the *mens rea* of intent but not recklessness, so reduces but does not remove fault. D will be guilty of the lesser crime, e.g. manslaughter instead of murder.
Self-defence	If D uses self-defence, there is no fault and the result is an acquittal. This applies even if D makes a mistake, as long as the mistake is genuine.

- The level of fault can be reflected in sentencing:
  - Mitigating and aggravating factors show a lesser or greater level of fault.
  - The sentence will then reflect this.
  - Even where the judge has no discretion in the sentence imposed, the tariff system recognises degrees of fault.
  - So that where there is a greater degree of fault, the recommended term will be higher.

Problems with fault in criminal law

- The thin skull rule means D may be liable due to a vulnerability in the victim rather than because of fault.
- Case example: in *Blaue*, V refused the operation which could have saved her life, but D was still liable for her death.

- D may be guilty of murder even if the intent is only to seriously injure, as in *DPP v Smith*:
  - This is a lower level of fault than intent to kill, but has the same consequence, a life sentence.
- The **OAPA** offences of **s 47 ABH**, and GBH under **s 20**, have a level of fault (*mens rea*) which does not match the *actus reus*:
  - D only needs to intend or see the risk of an assault or battery to be guilty of ABH.
  - D only needs to intend or see the risk of ABH to be guilty of GBH under **s 20**.
  - Both show a lower level of fault than the *actus reus* suggests.
- In *Gemmell and Richards*, the HL recognised the injustice of such a low level of fault (objective recklessness) leading to criminal liability, and changed the law.
- Gross negligence seems to be a lower level of fault than such a serious crime as manslaughter warrants.
- The offence of unlawful act manslaughter only requires *mens rea* for the unlawful act and not for the death, so D may be liable for manslaughter where there was only *mens rea* for a minor crime like criminal damage.

Now test yourself

Tested ☐

1 What is the fault element in criminal law?
2 How does the defence of intoxication reflect the degree of fault involved?
3 What change as regards fault did the HL make in *Gemmell and Richards*?
4 What effect might fault have on sentencing?

Answers on page 127

Strict liability in criminal law (liability without fault)

- This most often applies to regulatory offences.
- Examples include illegal parking, requirements for car insurance and tax, food safety, supply of drugs, pollution, etc.
- 'Real' crimes cause more controversy.
- Case example: The HL overturned the conviction in *Sweet v Parsley (1970)* because she had no knowledge that her premises were being used for drugs, so was not at fault.
- 'State of affairs' crimes do not require any fault at all; D can be liable just for being in the wrong place at the wrong time.
- Case example: In *Winzar*, a man was arrested for being drunk on a highway, although he had been put there by the police.

Should there be liability without fault in criminal law?

Yes	It protects the public.
Yes	Regulatory offences are minor and carry no social stigma.
Yes	The judge can address the issue of fault when sentencing.
No	It is arguably unjust to convict and punish someone without fault.
No	At the very least it means a criminal record, whatever the sentence.

Contract

- Fault is seen in contract law at various stages.
- Breach of contract:
  - The party in breach is seen as the one at fault and liable to pay damages.
- Misrepresentation:
  - Fraud is the highest level of fault – *Derry v Peek (1889)*.
  - Negligence is lower.
  - Even innocent misrepresentations will be actionable.
- Remedies will also reflect the degree of fault:
  - Damages are only awarded for foreseeable loss – *Hadley (1854)*.
  - Rescission is a discretionary remedy, and will not be awarded to a party that is at fault.

Tort

- Fault is a major element of tort law.
- It is seen in any breach of duty cases, where D has to reach the standard of a reasonable person, whether in negligence or under the Occupiers' Liability Act:
  - If the required standard is not met, D is in breach and will be liable.
  - However, D will not be at fault if sufficient precautions have been taken, as in *Bolton v Stone (1951)*.
  - Professionals have a higher duty, children a lower one (*Bolam 1957, Mullins 1998*) – this in some way recognises the different degrees of fault involved.
  - In *Nettleship v Weston*, a learner was expected to reach the standard of a competent driver even though it can be said that she had a lower level of fault because she was still learning.
- There is an element of fault seen in causation, as this requires foreseeability of harm:
  - D is not liable for damage which is too remote from the breach – *Wagon Mound (1961)*.
- In nuisance, the fault element is that D has 'unreasonably interfered' with someone's enjoyment:
  - Motive is not usually relevant in finding liability, but can be in nuisance if malice is shown.
  - Case examples: In *Christie v Davy (1893)*, the malice of one party to the dispute tipped the balance as to who was liable in nuisance. Malice was also a decisive factor in finding liability in *Hollywood Silver Fox Farm (1936)*.
- The defences of consent and contributory negligence recognise that if C is wholly or partly at fault the claim fails or damages are reduced.

Problems with fault in tort law

- The thin skull rule applies in civil law as well as crime and again can seem harsh, as in *Smith v Leech-Brain (1962)* where the fault of the employer (negligence) only caused minor harm, but he was liable for the cancer.

- Proving fault can be difficult and many victims are left without compensation, especially in medical negligence cases.
- The various tests for duty and breach mean the tort system is inconsistent in providing remedies.
- The possibility of introducing a no-fault system for traffic accidents was the subject of the Pearson Committee report, but in the main this has not been acted upon.

Now test yourself

Tested ☐

5 What is the fault element in the tort of negligence?
6 How does the rule that children are judged against a child of similar age rather than a reasonable adult reflect the level of fault involved?
7 How might the various breach factors affect whether fault is proved in negligence?
8 How does the defence of contributory negligence reflect the degree of fault involved?

Answers on page 127

Strict liability in tort (liability without fault)

- The main area of strict liability in tort is the rule under *Rylands v Fletcher*.
- However, liability has become less strict with the case of *Cambridge Water (1994)* because there must now be foreseeability of harm in *Rylands* cases, as for negligence.
- The Consumer Protection Act imposes strict liability on producers of goods:
  - This extends to others who are involved in production and distribution, all of whom may be liable even if not personally at fault.
- Also vicarious liability imposes liability without fault:
  - Vicarious liability cases can be used to show someone can be liable though not personally at fault, although it is not strict liability in the true sense because *someone* has to be at fault.

Should there be liability without fault in civil law?

Yes	It protects the public, e.g. under the Consumer Protection Act liability is strict so V may be saved the trouble and expense of a court case.
Yes	If a universal no-fault system was introduced, e.g. for road accidents, the state would pay, so every victim would get compensated even if D could not pay.
Yes	In vicarious liability cases the employer is better able to pay, so C is compensated for any harm.
No	In vicarious liability cases the employer may not be at fault but must pay for the wrongdoing of an employee.
No	D should pay only where they are at fault.
No	In a fault-based system the victim is fully compensated by the wrongdoer, whereas in a universal system the state would pay everyone but a lesser amount.

Check your understanding: 1

1 Add the appropriate defence to the column on the right.

Level of fault	Defence
Recognises D is not fully responsible due to an abnormality of mental functioning, so there is a reduced level of fault.	
D has lost control for a specified reason, so there is a reduced level of fault.	
D is not at fault at all because of a total loss of control.	
D is not fully responsible so there is a reduced level of fault and a special verdict.	
This can negate the *mens rea* of intent but not recklessness, so reduces but does not remove fault.	

Answers on page 127

Is fault an essential requirement of English law?

Revised ☐

Something that quite often comes up in examination questions is whether fault is an essential requirement of English law. The following table can be referred to when considering this question.

Fault is a requirement	Fault is not a requirement
Most crimes require that *actus reus* must be voluntary.	D can be liable even when not acting voluntarily in state-of-affairs offences.
Most crimes require *mens rea*.	Strict liability offences do not require *mens rea*.
The judge can consider aggravating and mitigating factors when sentencing.	The mandatory life sentence does not allow any discretion.
The tort of negligence looks at whether D has dropped below the standard of the reasonable person.	*Rylands v Fletcher* is a tort of strict liability so D is liable even if not negligent.
A manufacturer owes a duty to a consumer but is only liable if negligent.	Liability is strict under the Consumer Protection Act 1987 so D is liable even if not negligent.
If an employee is negligent they may be liable to compensate the person harmed.	However, an employer may be vicariously liable for that employee's negligence even though not personally at fault.

Exam tip

Whichever area you are studying, be sure to relate your case examples to the specific question. You will need to do more than explain fault and/or strict liability. You may be asked to consider how important fault is in proving liability or whether it is right to have liability without fault. Once you have found the focus of the question, use your cases to support your answer. Cases where you feel the outcome was unjust because D had a low level of fault may be useful. The next 'Check your understanding' box should help you with this.

Check your understanding: 2

2 Explain the fault element in the following three cases and whether it seems to be at the right level for liability to be imposed.

a) In *Stone and Dobinson*, the Ds had made some efforts to care for his sister, but were found guilty of manslaughter when she died from anorexia, because they had voluntarily taken on a duty to look after her.

b) In *Nedrick*, D was liable for unlawful act manslaughter when he set fire to a house and someone died, because he had the *mens rea* for arson and the *actus reus* of murder because he caused her death.

c) In *Nettleship v Weston*, a learner driver was liable in negligence because she had not reached the standard of a competent driver.

Answers on page 127

Summary

- ✔ Intention is the highest level of fault in criminal law.
- ✔ For most crimes the level of fault is subjective recklessness.
- ✔ Manslaughter can be committed by 'gross negligence'.
- ✔ Defences can reduce or even remove the fault element.
- ✔ Mitigating and aggravating factors indicate a decreased or increased amount of fault involved and can thus affect the sentence.
- ✔ Strict liability means there is no fault, but this mostly applies to regulatory offences.
- ✔ For 'real' crimes it is arguable that fault should always be needed.
- ✔ 'State of affairs' crimes do not require any fault at all; D can be liable just for being in the wrong place at the wrong time – *Winzar*.

- ✔ The main fault element in contract is breach of the agreement.
- ✔ Misrepresentation has various levels of fault.
- ✔ The main fault element in tort is negligence, not reaching the required standard of care.
- ✔ Professionals have a higher duty, children a lower one (*Bolam, Mullins*).
- ✔ There is an element of fault seen in causation, as this requires foreseeability of harm.
- ✔ In nuisance the fault element is that D has 'unreasonably interfered' with someone's enjoyment.
- ✔ Motive is not usually relevant in finding liability, but can be in nuisance if malice is shown – *Christie v Davy*.

Points for an essay

- The thin skull rule means D may be liable due to a vulnerability in the victim rather than because of fault – *Blaue*.
- D may be guilty of murder even if the intent is only to seriously injure – *DPP v Smith*.
- The **OAPA** offences of **s 47 ABH**, and **GBH** under **s 20**, have a lower level of fault (*mens rea*) than the *actus reus* suggests.
- *Gemmell and Richards* improved the law to avoid the injustice of such a low level of fault (objective recklessness) leading to criminal liability.
- Gross negligence for manslaughter seems to be a lower level of fault than such a serious crime warrants.
- The offence of unlawful act manslaughter only requires *mens rea* for the unlawful act and not for the death.
- Strict liability allows for liability without fault in both criminal and civil law.
- The thin skull rule applies in civil law as well as crime and again can seem harsh, as in *Smith v Leech-Brain*.
- Proving fault can be difficult in tort and many victims are left without compensation, especially in medical negligence cases.
- The various tests for duty and breach mean the tort system is inconsistent in providing remedies.

16 Balancing conflicting interests

Introduction

Interests are sometimes called rights. If we have a right to something, we can say we have an interest in it. With rights come corresponding duties, such as a right to be safe from harm and a duty not to cause harm, a right to property and a duty not to steal, etc. It works both ways, so if I have a right then you have a duty not to interfere with it and *vice versa*. If a right exists then it may need protecting or enforcing. The law may have to step in to consider whose rights have been interfered with and to try to balance those rights or interests in order to achieve a just outcome.

- In criminal law, we have a right not to be harmed and this imposes a corresponding duty on others not to cause harm.

- There is a similar right and duty in the tort of negligence.

- In contract law, a buyer has a right to receive goods or services and the other party to the contract has a corresponding duty to supply the goods or services.

- When these rights and interests conflict, the law must balance them and attempt to reach a just solution.

Balancing interests and justice   Revised ☐

Balancing conflicting interests is one way of trying to achieve justice, so some of the theories from Chapter 13 (pages 92–96) may be used when discussing interests which may conflict and how they should be balanced.

- A utilitarian, like Bentham, might say justice is best achieved by balancing the interests to ensure the greatest good for the greatest number.

- Mill would argue that the law should not interfere unless harm is caused to others.

- A theory which attempts to explain the importance of balancing interests and how justice is best achieved is that of Pound, who was an American lawyer:
  - Pound saw law as a tool which could engineer how society was regulated by balancing interests in order to build the best structure possible; thus it was a kind of social control
  - He believed that interests should only be balanced against other interests of the same kind.
  - Public interests should be balanced only against other public interests, and private against private.

Public and private interests

Although Pound argued that interests should only be balanced against other interests of the same kind, this has not been the case in practice. Examples of the public interest being in conflict with private interests are seen in many of the cases, especially those involving law and morals (see Chapter 12 pages 85–91).

Examples

- In abortion cases the rights of the child to be born conflict with the rights of the mother who is seeking an abortion; there are also public interest groups that argue for the right to life.
- In euthanasia cases some interest groups argue against the taking of a life and others favour the right of a person to choose whether and when to die.
- These groups reflect the views of a wider section of the public which may come into conflict with the individual interests of the person concerned.
- Other examples include the right to medical treatment (especially where expensive drugs are needed) and the right to refuse such treatment (especially where the refusal of treatment may result in death).
- These cases end up in court because there is a conflict between the various interests, not just the parties immediately involved but the wider interests of society as a whole.
- The law must make an effort to balance these and achieve an outcome which is fair to all the parties involved.

Now test yourself

Tested ☐

1 What were the different interests in *Re A* (see the case example on page 95) and how did they conflict?
2 How did the court balance those interests?
3 Which theory of justice was dominant in the case?

Answers on pages 127–28

Other times when public and private interests conflict are when public policy considerations are involved.

- Examples include proving a duty of care in tort:
  - A duty is not imposed unless it is 'fair, just and reasonable' to do so.
  - A case example is *Hill v CC of West Yorkshire (1988)* where the police did not owe a duty because it was not in the public interest and could make policing less effective.
  - The victim's private interest is subordinated to the public interest in such cases.
- Nuisance cases involve private interests conflicting (so are a good source for any discussion of this area) but even here the public interest can be seen.

Case example

In *Miller v Jackson*, a woman found cricket balls commonly landing in her garden to be a nuisance. She won her case in nuisance against the cricket club. The courts have a discretion in whether to grant an injunction or not and this allowed the court to engineer a balance by refusing an injunction. Her interest (in a quiet life) was subordinated to the public interest (in a social and sporting activity).

- In criminal law, the public interest in protecting society has to be balanced against the rights of D to a fair trial, access to a lawyer, bail and other procedures intended to achieve a fairer balance between the state and the individual.

● The defence of intoxication balances the public interest in protecting people from drunken criminals and D's interest in not being guilty if incapable of forming *mens rea*:
  – The rules from *Majewski (1976)* mean that in crimes of specific intent, the private interest prevails and the defence applies (to reduce the crime to one of basic intent).
  – In basic intent crimes, the public interest prevails and the defence fails.
● It is against public policy that intoxication should fully excuse a criminal act.

Case examples

In *O'Grady (1987)*, while intoxicated D hit his friend over the head in the mistaken belief that the friend was trying to kill him. His friend died and he was convicted of manslaughter. The CA said:

'There are two competing interests. On the one hand the interest of the defendant who has only acted according to what he believed to be necessary to protect himself, and on the other hand that of the public in general, and the victim in particular who, probably through no fault of his own, has been injured or perhaps killed because of the defendant's drunken mistake. Reason recoils from the conclusion that in such circumstances a defendant is entitled to leave the court without a stain on his character.'

In *Dowds*, D had been drinking when he attacked his partner with a knife and killed her. The judge said:

'… public policy proceeds on the basis that a defendant who voluntarily takes alcohol and behaves in a way in which he might not have behaved when sober is not normally entitled to be excused from the consequences of his actions.'

Both cases show that the public interest (in not allowing drunkenness to excuse violence) is the dominant interest, and will usually mean the defence is rejected.

Now test yourself

Tested ☐

4 What does Pound mean by saying that law is an engineering tool?
5 How would a utilitarian engineer the balance between conflicting interests?
6 What is the dominant interest in cases involving intoxication?
7 Give one example from the substantive law and one from the legal process and explain what interests are in conflict.

Answers on page 128

Exam tip

It is important not only to explain the nature of the conflicting interests in a case, but also how your chosen case illustrates how these are balanced. In *Miller*, for example, you could say that the interests of the parties (Mrs Miller and the cricket club) were in conflict, and so too were the interests of Mrs Miller and the public. The discretion of the court as to whether to grant an injunction was a tool used to engineer a balance between these competing interests, and the public interest prevailed.

Balancing interests and human rights

● In human rights law there are often public and private interests in conflict:
  – Individual rights and freedoms are protected by the **European Convention on Human Rights**, but this allows for exceptions (called 'derogations') in the public interest, e.g. where state security is involved
  – The individual has rights but these may be sacrificed for the public good.
  – A utilitarian would probably support the balance being tipped towards the public good as this theory has little time for individual rights.
  – Some of the law on human rights involves a conflict in itself, e.g. one person's right to freedom of speech may conflict with another's right to a private life or not to be abused in the media or in employment situations.

- The law attempts to protect people's interests and rights but getting the right balance is not always easy.
- In protecting one person's interest, another person's may be forfeited. This means any balancing act may not achieve justice for all the parties, as in *Miller v Jackson*, where she felt she did not get justice because an award of damages did not help with her problem.

How can the law balance interests which are in conflict?

- By punishing those who break the law, thus protecting the public in general.
- By providing for defences as well as offences, e.g. the defences of loss of control, automatism, insanity, etc. help to protect D's interests.
- By protecting weaker parties against businesses, e.g. the Consumer Protection Act and the Sale of Goods Act, which help to protect the interests of the individual consumer by imposing strict liability on the manufacturer or seller of goods.
- By providing a fair legal system, e.g. access to justice, use of juries, rules of PACE, Bail Act, rules of evidence, etc. which help to protect D's interests against the state.
- By providing the institutions, such as courts and tribunals which, if conflicts of interest arise, will attempt to balance them as fairly as possible.

Check your understanding: 1

1 What types of interest were in conflict in *Miller v Jackson*?
2 In what way did these interests conflict?
3 How was the conflict resolved?
4 Was justice achieved according to utilitarianism?
5 Was justice achieved in your opinion?

Answers on page 128

Typical mistake

Students often fail to refer to the public interest in discussing the conflict and merely give examples of conflicts which arise between private interests, e.g. claimant/defendant and/or claimant/victim. The case examples table below and over the page should help you avoid this mistake.

Exam tip

Try to consider the wider impact on society and discuss interests outside the obvious examples above. You could note that private interests are sometimes in conflict with public interests and in some cases are subordinated to those of the community (see the case examples table below and over the page). Balancing interests to achieve the best for society as a whole can be seen in the utilitarian theory of maximising happiness.

Cases

Case	Brief facts	Which private interests were in conflict?	Was there also a public interest?	How was the conflict resolved?
Bolton v Stone (1951)	A woman was hit by a cricket ball while walking near a cricket ground.	The interests of the cricket club (to be able to play) and the woman (not to have her enjoyment spoiled).	The public has an interest in having sporting activities in the community.	The court decided the club had done enough to avoid the risks so was not liable. The public interest helped tip the balance in favour of the club.
Latimer v AEC (1886)	A worker was hurt when he slipped after some flooding in a factory.	The interests of the factory owner (in keeping the factory open after a flood) and the employee (to receive compensation for his injury).	The public had an interest in not closing the factory which would affect both the workers and consumers.	The court decided the owner had done enough to avoid the risks so was not liable. The public interest helped tip the balance in favour of keeping the factory open.

Case	Brief facts	Which private interests were in conflict?	Was there also a public interest?	How was the conflict resolved?
Quintavalle (2005)	A couple wanted to choose an embryo that would be a match for their son who needed a transplant.	The interests of the couple (in helping their son get a transplant) and those of their son (in having a better quality of life) conflicted with those of Ms Quintavalle who represented a pressure group who were against such treatment because it was not ethical.	The public interest in what many believe is immoral (discarding unwanted embryos) and the conflicting public interest of having freedom of choice for the many people who may want to choose an embryo for various medical reasons.	The court ruled that choosing an embryo was possible under the law. On balance the law was in favour of allowing choice in certain circumstances.
Brown (1994)	A group of men performed sado-masochistic acts on each other, causing serious harm.	The individual interests in the freedom to do as you will in private.	The public interest (in prohibiting immoral behaviour) and the conflicting public interest (in having freedom of choice).	The court ruled that consent was no defence so the possible effect of immoral behaviour on society as a whole outweighed the private interests of the individuals to consent to harm.

Typical mistake

There is a clear overlap between the various concepts of law and students sometimes fail to focus on the correct area. *Re A* is an example of the overlap. There was a conflict of interests between the different parties as well as the public interest. There was also a question of whether it was immoral to take a life. Finally, the utilitarian theory of justice was seen in the decision of the court, but under the natural law theory justice was not achieved. It is quite acceptable to use the same case in different examination answers, but be sure to focus your answer on the particular concept referred to in the question.

Check your understanding: 2

6 Complete the columns on the right with a brief explanation of how interests might conflict and whether you think the law has been successful in balancing the conflicting interests. The first is done for you as an example.

The interest	The conflict	The success of the law
Freedom of expression	There is often a conflict between individual rights or freedoms as one person's freedom may interfere with another's, as in freedom of speech and the right not to be defamed. There is also the public interest in keeping state secrets which will be in conflict with the interests of those who believe in openness.	The law has been quite successful in the attempt to balance private interests by incorporating the **European Convention on Human Rights**, but also having laws against defamation. The law in relation to the private vs. the public interest has been less successful as many believe that governments need to be more open with the public, but the law has protected the public interest in many cases where an individual has leaked information.
Donoghue v Stevenson and the Consumer Protection Act 1987		
The mandatory sentence for murder		
Anti-terrorism laws which allow people to be detained without charge		

Answers on page 128

Summary

- Rights and corresponding duties in criminal law:
  - A right to life, a duty not to kill (murder, manslaughter cases).
  - A right to own property, a duty not to steal it (theft, robbery, burglary).
- Rights and corresponding duties in tort:
  - A right not to be harmed, a duty not to harm (negligence cases, e.g. *Donoghue*).
  - A right to 'reasonable enjoyment', a duty not to interfere with that enjoyment (nuisance).
- Where interests are in conflict, the law will try to engineer a balance which will achieve social cohesion.
- For Pound, interests should be balanced to achieve a well-structured society.
- Public and private interests should not be balanced against each other.
- For a utilitarian, a just outcome to any balancing act would be to maximise happiness.
- The purpose of law is to satisfy as many interests as possible.
- Any attempt to balance interests on different levels would mean the dominant interest prevails and this is likely to be the public one.

Points for an essay

Again, although there is a similarity between questions there is usually a different emphasis. You will need to pick out the particular issues that you are being asked to focus on, but the following is a guide to what you need to be able to do.

- Identify what interests are and how they may correspond to duties.
- Explain Pound's theory that the law can be used to engineer how society behaves:
  - Note that Pound did not agree that private interests should be balanced against public ones.
  - In most cases where public and private interests are in conflict it is the public interest that will prevail, so Pound's point is a good one.
- Consider how and when interests can conflict and relate this to other areas of study:
  - the legal process
  - the various legal institutions
  - the substantive law (crime, contract and tort).
- Consider how the law balances various interests which are in conflict.
- Consider whether the law has achieved a fair balance when attempting to balance those interests.
- Consider how the theories of justice may apply to how the law may engineer a balance:
  - A utilitarian would want any balancing of interests to maximise happiness and to achieve the greatest benefit overall.
  - Mill would want to see a minimum of interference with people's interests unless the law needs to act to prevent harm to others.
  - A natural law follower would want the public interest to prevail where there is an issue of morality.
- Illustrate a discussion of conflicting interests with cases and examples.
- Depending on the focus of the particular question you may need to evaluate the extent to which the law is effective and/or successful in engineering a fair balance, or you may need to discuss the difficulties of achieving a fair balance:
  - Use case examples to show whether the law has got the balance right.
  - Note that the law may be less effective/successful when balancing private against public interests.
  - Note that difficulties arise in any cases with a moral element (see earlier examples).

Exam practice

AQA June 2012

Explain what is meant by 'balancing conflicting interests'. Discuss the extent to which English law balances conflicting interests and briefly consider whether it is important to do so. [30 marks + 5 marks for AO3]

Answers online

Online

Answers

Chapter 1

Now test yourself

1 The three 'C's are:

   a) conduct

   b) circumstances

   c) consequences.

2 An omission can amount to *actus reus* when there is a duty to act.

3 Miller was liable for what appears to be an accident because he had created the situation so had a duty to do something about it.

4 Applying the rule on factual causation to *Pagett*, we can say that but for *Pagett* holding the girl in front of him while shooting at police she would not have died.

5 Applying the rules on legal causation to *Pagett*, we could say that his act in shooting at police made a significant contribution to her death and the police returning fire was foreseeable so did not break the chain of causation.

6 a) A refusal of hospital treatment would not usually break the chain of causation but there may be an exception if the decision had no reasonable foundation.

   b) Poor hospital treatment would not usually break the chain of causation but there may be an exception if it was independent of D's act and a potent cause in itself.

   c) Running away from an attack would not usually break the chain of causation but there may be an exception if it is a 'daft' reaction.

7 The first part of the *Woollin* test is that death or serious injury is virtually certain.

8 In *Stringer*, a fire started at the bottom of the stairs when people are asleep is certain to cause at least serious injury.

9 The second part of the *Woollin* test is that D appreciates that death or serious injury is virtually certain.

10 In *Stringer*, it is arguable that his age and low IQ meant he did not appreciate that death or serious injury was virtually certain, but the jury may well find intent because it must have been clear even to the boy that the fire was virtually certain to cause serious injury, if not death.

11

Case	Principle
Fagan (1986)	An act may be seen as continuing.
Stone and Dobinson (1977)	Liability for an omission arises if there is a duty of responsibility for someone.
Roberts (1971)	A foreseeable act of the victim will not break the chain of causation.
Cheshire (1991)	D must make a significant contribution to the result plus hospital treatment won't break the chain of causation unless independent of D's act.

Case	Principle
Blaue (1975)	D must take the victim as found so is liable for the full consequences.
DPP v Smith (1960)	The *mens rea* for murder is intent to kill or seriously injure.

Check your understanding: 1 Application practice

1 A result crime is where a particular consequence, or result, is part of the *actus reus*. This is significant because it must be shown that D caused that result in fact and in law.

2 Pagett factually caused death because '**but for**' his action the girl would not have died (*White*). He also made a '**significant contribution**' (*Cheshire*) to her death. The intervening act of the police shooting back was **foreseeable** and so did not break the **chain of causation** (*Roberts*). He therefore also legally caused death, so had the *actus reus* of murder. It was probably (it isn't 100 per cent clear) not Pagett's **aim** to **kill or seriously injure** the girl so there is no *mens rea* of direct intent. We have to ask whether death or serious injury was a '**virtual certainty**' and if D **appreciated** this (*Nedrick*). If the jury believe that Pagett intended to kill or seriously injure the police, whether directly or by appreciating it as a virtual certainty, then the principle of **transferred malice** means that this intent is transferred from them to the girl, and he may be found guilty of murder. If the jury do not find that he appreciated death or serious injury as virtually certain then there is no indirect intent. He will probably be found not guilty of murder due to lack of *mens rea*. (He will be guilty of unlawful act manslaughter; see Chapter 3.)

Check your understanding: 2 Essay practice

3 One argument against having a mandatory life sentence for murder is that it allows the judge no discretion in sentencing, so the circumstances of the killing cannot be taken into account.

4 The Law Commission recommendations would change the approach to sentencing in a case where D intended to cause serious harm but not to kill, because they recommended that this would be second-degree murder with a discretionary sentence.

5 The Law Commission recommendations would not change the approach to sentencing in euthanasia cases, because in such cases there is a killing with clear intent so this would be first-degree murder and carry a mandatory life sentence.

Chapter 2

Now test yourself

1 The Coroners and Justice Act 2009 applies to murder.

2 The three things which need to be proved for **s 54** are:

   a) that D lost self-control

   b) the loss of self-control was triggered by something specified in **s 55**

   c) that a normal person of D's sex and age would have reacted in the same way in D's circumstances.

3 The qualifying triggers are:

a) D's fear of serious violence from V against D or another identified person; or

b) a thing or things done or said (or both) which:

(i) constituted circumstances of an extremely grave character, and

(ii) caused D to have a justifiable sense of being seriously wronged

c) or a combination of both of these.

4 The Act specifically excludes sexual infidelity as a qualifying trigger.

5 The Act says the defence is not allowed if D acted in a 'considered desire for revenge'.

Check your understanding: 1 Application practice

1 The defence may still fail on the facts of *Ibrams and Gregory*. They had been 'terrorised' so there was a qualifying trigger (fear of serious violence). However, although there is now no need for the loss of self-control to be sudden, any time delay may indicate that there was no loss of control at all. It could also indicate a 'considered desire for revenge' and so be excluded by **s 54 (4)**. Finally, it may fail because even if there was a loss of control at the start, it is unlikely to have caused D to kill several days later, so the killing did not 'result from' the loss of control as required by **s 54 (1)**.

Now test yourself

6 *Clinton* – sexual infidelity may be relevant to the circumstances of D, even though excluded by **s 55**.

7 *Byrne* – an 'abnormality of mind' (now mental functioning) for diminished responsibility is one that reasonable people would term abnormal.

8 *Tandy* – an abnormality caused by alcoholism may be accepted as diminished responsibility (also stated in *Wood*).

9 *Lloyd* – impairment of responsibility need not be total but must be more than trivial.

10 *Dietschmann* – where there is evidence of intoxication as well as another cause of 'abnormality' the jury should ignore the intoxication.

Check your understanding: 2 Application practice

2 Mrs Freaney was charged with murder and pleaded diminished responsibility.

3 If successful, the defence reduces the charge to manslaughter and this is important because it gives the judge discretion in sentencing.

4 That D was suffering from an abnormality of mental functioning which:

a) arose from a recognised medical condition

b) substantially impaired D's ability to do one or more of the things mentioned in subsection (1A)

c) provides an explanation for D's act or omission.

5 The three things that might be impaired are the ability:

a) to understand the nature of D's conduct

b) to form a rational judgement

c) to exercise self-control.

6 Under the Coroners and Justice Act 2009 **s 52**, she would need to show that she was suffering from an 'abnormality of mental functioning' at the time of the killing. In *Byrne*, it was said that 'abnormality of mind' meant a state of mind so different from that of normal human beings that the reasonable man would deem it abnormal, and the same is likely to apply to abnormality of mental functioning. The abnormality must arise from a 'recognised medical condition', which would be her severe stress. She will then need to convince the jury that the abnormality of mental functioning substantially impaired her ability to do one of the three things set out in **s 52**. In *Lloyd*, the court held that 'substantial' did not mean 'total' but was more than 'trivial'. She seemed to understand the nature of her conduct, but it is possible she could not form a rational judgement due to the stress. Possibly she was also unable to exercise self-control at the time of the killing, but only one of the three things need apply. The abnormality of mental functioning seems to have caused, or at least significantly contributed to, the killing of her son. Her plea of diminished responsibility is likely to succeed under the new law, so she would be convicted of manslaughter not murder.

Check your understanding: 3 Essay practice

7 You may have chosen different points, but here are three examples:

- Where there is evidence of intoxication as well as another cause of 'abnormality' the jury has to perform an almost impossible task of separating the one from the other (*Dietschmann*). This means that if D is drunk and also has an abnormality, for example post-traumatic stress, the jury must consider whether the stress has sufficiently impaired D's responsibility and try to ignore the intoxication. This may be very difficult if the evidence is that D killed because of the drink as well as the stress.

- The Law Commission had suggested removing any need for loss of self-control but this was rejected. This means cases such as *Thornton* and *Ahluwalia* may still fail as in those cases the women had calmed down before they acted. In *Thornton*, she went into the kitchen for some time and then picked up a knife and stabbed him, and in *Ahluwalia*, she waited until he was asleep. Although there is no longer a need for any loss of control to be 'sudden', as was the case before the reforms, so this is an improvement in the law, these facts indicate that there was no loss of control at all and the new law will therefore probably not change the result.

- The burden of proof is on D for diminished responsibility. This does not seem fair because in most other defences, including loss of control, D only has to raise the issue and the prosecution has to disprove it. Arguably this should also apply to diminished responsibility.

Chapter 3

Now test yourself

1 Stone and Dobinson had a voluntary duty of responsibility.

2 Pittwood had a contractual duty.

3 Gibbins had a duty of relationship as a parent and Proctor had a voluntary duty of responsibility.

Check your understanding: 1 Application practice

1
- Risk of death: It is known that ecstasy can kill so there is a risk of death.
- Duty: they owed her a duty as a visitor and/or as a child in their care.
- Breach: They did not call an ambulance for some time; similarly to *Stone and Dobinson* they had breached their duty to her by not taking reasonable care.
- Gross negligence: This could go either way. They had hidden the tablets and had attempted to treat her, so the jury may not think this was sufficiently negligent to be 'gross'. However, they did not call an ambulance for some time which could be gross negligence.

On these facts the jury found that they had not shown a sufficiently high level of negligence to be deemed criminal so they were not guilty of gross negligence manslaughter.

Now test yourself

4 In *Nedrick*, the unlawful act was arson (a type of criminal damage).

5 In *Woollin*, the throwing of the baby was unlawful – a type of assault.

6 In *Pagett*, shooting at the police was the unlawful act.

7 Cato was found guilty but Dalby was found not guilty.

8 The essential difference between the cases is that in *Cato* D not only supplied but assisted the V to take heroin, whereas in *Dalby* V injected himself.

9 The defence would have relied on *Dalby* in *Kennedy*.

10 The prosecution would have relied on *Cato*.

11 Kennedy was found guilty at his trial.

12 The House of Lords held that supplying drugs was not enough if D did not participate in the taking of them.

13 The House of Lords' decision followed *Dalby*.

Check your understanding: 2 Application practice

2 In *Nedrick*, a reasonable person would see a risk of some harm resulting from setting fire to a residential house and the fire directly caused the death of the child; there was nothing that broke the chain of causation.

3 In *Woollin*, a reasonable person would see a risk of some harm resulting from throwing a baby across a room and again nothing broke the chain of causation.

4 In *Pagett*, a reasonable person would see a risk of some harm resulting from shooting at the police and although it could be argued that the police returning fire caused the death, this action was foreseeable so did not break the chain of causation between D shooting at them and the death of the girl.

Check your understanding: 3 Application practice

5 In *Nedrick*, the *mens rea* was either intent or subjective recklessness to cause criminal damage. He must have at least

seen the risk of causing damage by fire but continued in his actions, so had *mens rea*.

6 In *Woollin*, the *mens rea* was either intent or subjective recklessness to cause serious harm (we know this because he was charged with murder); he may not have intended to cause serious harm but must have realised the risk of it.

7 In *Pagett*, the *mens rea* was either intent or subjective recklessness to shoot at the police. It is not clear which type of assault the unlawful act would be but even an assault or battery would be enough. So as long as he saw the risk of causing the police to apprehend violence, or he saw the risk of applying force on the police, then he has *mens rea*.

Chapter 4

Now test yourself

1 a) Stalking someone amounted to assault in *Constanza*.

b) Silent phone calls amounted to assault in *Ireland*.

2 Touching someone's clothes was said to be unlawful force in *Thomas*.

3 a) The battery was applying unlawful force by driving onto the police officer's foot.

b) The principle in regard to *actus reus* was that an act could be continuing.

c) This was treated as a continuing act of battery (driving the car onto the police officer's foot and then leaving it there) rather than an omission (not moving off).

Check your understanding: 1 Application practice

1 In *Roberts*, he committed the *actus reus* of battery when he touched her coat. This is unlawful force as shown in *Thomas*. He clearly intended to grab her coat so he had the *mens rea* for the battery. All that remains to be proved is that his actions caused (occasioned) some harm. There is no need to prove he intended or was reckless as to any harm occurring. As he made a significant contribution to her injuries the only issue is whether she broke the chain of causation by jumping out of the car. As this is a foreseeable reaction for a young woman who is scared it will not. He is therefore guilty of ABH.

Now test yourself

4
- A bruise is likely to be a battery as it is fairly trivial (*Chan Fook*).
- Several bruises – probably ABH **s 47** but could be **s 20** if, for example, on a young child, as decided in *Bollom*.
- A fractured skull – this is serious harm (*Saunders*) so would be **s 20** or **s 18** grievous bodily harm depending on *mens rea*.
- A small cut, although technically a wound, is likely to be charged as ABH **s 47** as in *Savage*.
- A large gash is serious so would be **s 20** or **s 18** wounding.
- A broken bone is serious enough for **s 20** or **s 18** grievous bodily harm.

Exam practice answers and quick quizzes at **www.therevisionbutton.co.uk/myrevisionnotes**

- A grazed knee is likely to be a battery if it is fairly trivial (*Chan Fook*) but if it was more serious could be **s 47** (*Roberts*).
- Internal injuries are probably serious so would be **s 20** or **s 18** grievous bodily harm depending on *mens rea*.

5

Brief facts	Principle	Case
Stalking a woman caused fear of force.	Silence may be enough for an assault.	*Constanza (1997)*
Case needed for principle only.	If D has *mens rea* for some harm that will be enough for **s 20**; there is no need to have *mens rea* for serious harm.	*Mowatt (1968)*
Case needed for principle only.	Grievous means serious harm.	*Saunders (1985)*
Silent telephone calls to women caused fear.	Words or even silence may be enough for an assault.	*Ireland (1997)*
A boy put acid in a dryer and another boy was injured.	A battery can be via another person.	*DPP v K (1990)*
A woman threw a glass of beer at another woman.	For ABH there is no need to foresee the risk of harm – only of an assault (or battery).	*Savage (1991)*
D placed his hand on the hilt of his sword and said if it was not assize time I would not take such language.	Words may prevent an assault by indicating it will not occur.	*Turbeville v Savage (1669)*
A man locked in a room got in a panic and was injured trying to get out.	Mere emotions such as fear, distress or panic are not enough for actual bodily harm; nor is trivial harm.	*Chan Fook (1994)*
A man grabbed a girl's coat and she was injured when she jumped from the car.	A foreseeable act by the victim will not break the chain of causation.	*Roberts*
A boy was hit in the eye by a pellet.	Wound means an open cut.	*C v Eisenhower (1983)*

Check your understanding: 2 Application practice

2 Battery is the most appropriate offence. Sergio 'grabbed at Sandy's jacket' and touching clothes can amount to battery (*Thomas*). A graze does not seem enough for **s 47** assault occasioning actual bodily harm, but it is a possible alternative; there is a battery which has caused harm (a graze) and in *DPP v Smith* even cutting someone's hair was said to amount to bodily harm. Finally, even though the skin is broken (*Eisenhower*) it is not likely to be seen as serious

enough to amount to wounding under **s 20**. Sergio is guilty of battery and probably of **s 47** ABH.

3 It may be assault if Sam was in fear of immediate personal violence. It would be a question of whether he saw it coming and as he 'jumped aside' it appears he did. If the book hit him it would be battery. It is an indirect battery (*Haystead*) on the elderly woman which appears to have resulted in harm as she 'cried out in pain'. If the harm is more than trivial (*Chan Fook*) Tracey can be liable under **s 47**. She need not intend any harm. It is enough that she intended the battery (*Savage*). An alternative approach would be to use the principle of transferred malice (*Latimer*). She had the *mens rea* for a battery on Sam and this can be transferred to the woman.

4 The fact that the woman had 'brittle bones' suggests the thin skull rule applies (*Blaue*) so Tracey can be liable for the full results of her original action. Broken bones will be serious harm (*Saunders*) so it appears that it could be GBH **s 20**. However, for that she needs to have intended, or at least been reckless as to some harm (*Mowatt*), and this may be hard to prove. It is probably more appropriate to charge her under **s 47**; she has *mens rea* for a battery on Sam and the *actus reus* of causing harm to the elderly woman. The act of Sam jumping out of the way is foreseeable so it does not break the chain of causation (*Roberts*).

5 This could be assault, assuming that Viktor apprehended harm, i.e. is frightened by the threat. Words or even silence can amount to assault (*Ireland*). The problem is whether the fear is of 'immediate' harm. It is clear from both *Smith* and *Ireland* that 'immediate' is interpreted widely, but as it says the train 'pulled out of the station' this means it was leaving the station and so Viktor will not be in fear of immediate harm, so an assault charge is unlikely to succeed.

6 The skin is clearly broken (*Eisenhower*) so this amounts to wounding under **s 18** or **s 20**. The use of a knife suggests that serious harm was intended, especially as it says 'pulled out a knife' showing she had it with her. Steffi therefore has both *actus reus* and *mens rea* for **s 18**, wounding with intent, but if there was any problem with proving that she intended serious harm then the conviction may be for **s 20** instead.

> **Exam tip**
>
> Note that in every answer there is at least a brief reference to the given facts. This is really important as it shows the examiner that you have picked up on specific facts and have a good enough knowledge of the law to select only what is relevant.

Check your understanding: 3 Essay practice

7 The Law Commission recognised that the Offences Against the Person Act is outdated.

8 A problem with the structure of the Act is that the differences between the offences under **s 47**, **s 18**, and **s 20** are not clearly spelt out.

9 The problem regarding sentencing is that the offence in **s 20** has the same maximum sentence as **s 47** but is a much more serious offence.

10 The LC says the *actus reus* for **s 18** and **s 20** appears to be the same apart from a very slight difference in wording and it is 'notoriously difficult' to draw a distinction between 'causing' and 'inflicting'.

11 The main aims of the new project are to restructure the law, perhaps by creating a hierarchy of offences, and to modernise and simplify the language.

12 Whether the reforms will help, if they are implemented, is a matter of opinion. However, it is widely recognised that there are problems so the reforms will most probably be welcomed by those people dealing with the law. There is a clear need for modernisation and simplification of the outdated language. It also seems wrong that the sentencing for **s 20** and **s 47** has the same maximum so reform here is much needed. The three statutory offences overlap and there is no clear distinction drawn to highlight the differences between them. This is not the first time the LC has proposed changes, however, and the earlier report (No 218) was produced in 1993 but was never enacted; there is no guarantee that the new proposals will receive parliamentary time.

Chapter 5

Now test yourself

1

Case	Brief facts	Principle
Clarke (1972)	She absentmindedly took items from a supermarket shelf.	Temporary absentmindedness is not a defect of reason.
Windle (1952)	D killed his wife with an overdose but his words showed he knew his actions were legally wrong.	The insanity defence fails if D knows the act is legally wrong.
Kemp (1956)	D attacked his wife with a hammer due to a disease which reduced the flow of blood to the brain.	It was an internal factor which caused the defect of reason, so insanity.
Quick (1973)	A diabetic failed to eat after taking insulin and assaulted a patient.	It was an external factor which caused the defect of reason, so not insanity.
Hennessey (1983)	A diabetic failed to take his insulin and this had caused him to lose control of his actions.	It was an internal factor which caused the defect of reason, so insanity.
Sullivan (1984)	D hit out at someone during an epileptic fit.	It was an internal factor which caused the defect of reason, so insanity.
Burgess (1991)	D hit V over the head with a bottle when sleepwalking.	It was an internal factor which caused the defect of reason, so insanity.
Johnson (2007)	D forced his way into a neighbour's flat and stabbed him.	D knew the act was legally wrong, so the insanity defence failed.

2

Case	Brief facts	Principle
Bratty (1963)	D killed a girl with a stocking during an epileptic fit.	Lord Denning provided the definition of automatism as 'any mental disorder which has manifested itself in violence and is prone to recur'.
Lipman (1970)	D killed his girlfriend while under the influence of LSD.	Self-induced automatism means the defence fails.
Bailey (1983)	A diabetic hit someone with an iron bar after failing to eat.	Loss of control must be total and self-induced automatism means the defence fails.
Hardie (1984)	D set fire to a bedroom after taking Valium.	Taking sedatives will not exclude the defence; taking unpredictable drugs will.
A-G's Reference (No 2 of 1992) (1994)	D killed two people when his lorry crashed into a car.	Loss of control must be total.

Check your understanding: 1 Insanity and automatism

1 Insanity: A person may not be criminally liable because of their mental condition at the time they committed an alleged offence.

2 Automatism: A person might not be criminally liable because they lacked conscious control of their actions at the time of committing the alleged offence for a reason other than their mental condition.

3 The four main criticisms are:

   a) It is not clear whether the defence of insanity is even available in all cases.

   b) The law lags behind psychiatric understanding, and this partly explains why, in practice, the defence is underused and medical professionals do not apply the correct legal test.

   c) The label of 'insane' is outdated as a description of those with mental illness, and simply wrong as regards those who have learning disabilities or learning difficulties, or those with epilepsy.

   d) The case law on insane and non-insane automatism is incoherent and produces results that run counter to common sense.

4 No, there are fewer than 30 per year.

Check your understanding: 2 Application practice

5 If he pleads insanity, then under the *M'Naghten* rules he will have to show (the burden of proof is on D) that he had a defect of reason caused by a disease of the mind so that he did not know the nature and quality of his act or did not know it was legally wrong. He had a defect of reason as he was hallucinating, and he did not know 'the nature

and quality' of his act because he thought he was fighting snakes. However, the defect was caused by the LSD not a 'disease of the mind' and as this is an external factor it is not insanity.

He could plead automatism which would be better, as if successful it results in an acquittal. This requires that D has lost control and this must be total (*A-G's Reference No 2*). The problem with this defence is that self-induced automatism means the defence fails. Unlike in *Hardie*, where the defence succeeded because he had taken drugs which were meant to calm him, *Lipman* took an unpredictable drug so will not succeed with this defence.

Finally, he can argue intoxication. His intoxication was voluntary so the *Majewski* rules apply. This means he can use the defence if the crime is one of specific intent, which murder is. He didn't intend to kill or seriously injure his girlfriend so does not have the *mens rea* for murder. However, according to *Majewski* as the intoxication was voluntary he will be guilty of the related basic intent crime, which is manslaughter.

Now test yourself

3 Self-defence was rejected in *Martin* because the force was excessive.

4 You can rely on a mistaken belief to justify using force.

5 A case in support is *Williams (Gladstone) (1987)*.

6 You cannot rely on a mistake made due to intoxication.

7 A case in support is *O'Grady*.

8 The result of a successful plea of self-defence is an acquittal.

Check your understanding: 3 Application practice for self-defence

6 You can use self-defence if you can convince the jury that you genuinely believed the man to be attacking you. This belief can be mistaken (*Williams* and **s 76**), as long as it was not caused by intoxication. **S 76 (3)** provides that whether the force is reasonable is decided by reference to the circumstances as you believed them to be. Your mistake need not be reasonable either, as long as it was genuinely held – **s 76 (4)**.

7 This can also be self-defence, which includes defence of another, or it could be prevention of a crime. This latter defence comes from **s 3 (1)** of the Criminal Law Act 1967, which states: 'A person may use such force as is reasonable in the circumstances in the prevention of crime'. The same rules apply to both defences and you only need to show that the degree of force was reasonable. In these circumstances, you only pulled her away and the jury are likely to see this as reasonable force, unlike in *Martin* where the force was excessive.

Check your understanding: 4 Application practice for consent

8 It was said in *A-G's Reference (No 6 of 1980) (1981)* that there is implied consent in 'properly conducted games and sports'. The fact that he was sent off indicates that he was acting outside the rules, so arguably the sport was not 'properly conducted'. However in *Barnes*, the court held that only conduct that was sufficiently grave to be deemed criminal would mean the defence failed in sporting cases. The court

also said that this did not apply if the injury was caused intentionally. We know the charge is GBH under **s 20** so this would indicate that Jack has caused serious harm but he did not do so intentionally, which would be **s 18**. The defence should succeed.

9 It was said in *A-G's Reference (No 6 of 1980)* that implied consent applies to 'reasonable surgical interference'. In *Wilson* the defence was allowed when D branded his wife's buttocks. In that case the wife consented and it is not clear here, but there is no evidence to suggest that Lita did not consent to having her nose pierced. The question is whether she consented to harm, because in *Dica* the defence failed on this point. The infection is 'serious' so again the defence could fail because the harm was both serious and intentional. The court may feel the situation is near enough to *Wilson* to follow that case; if so, Tom will succeed in the defence. A final point is that it does not say how old Lita is. In *Burrell and Harmer*, boys of twelve and thirteen were not held to have consented to ABH caused by tattooing. If Lita is young this could be followed and the defence could fail.

10 Although Diane consents to her death it was made clear in *Pretty* that you cannot consent to murder. If her husband helps her die he cannot use the defence of consent to any charge that is brought.

Chapter 6

Now test yourself

1 Wild plants can be classed as property if taken for 'reward or sale or other commercial purpose'.

2 Animals can be classed as property if they have been tamed or kept in captivity.

3 *Gomez* followed *Lawrence* on the issue of consent.

4 Money and a television were appropriated in *Hinks*.

5 The girl was guilty of theft in *Davidge v Burnett* because she had been given the money for a particular purpose but spent it on Christmas presents instead.

6 The travel agent was not guilty of theft in *Hall* because the money had not been given for a particular purpose.

Check your understanding

1 a) There is probably no intent to permanently deprive, **s 6 (1)**. However, this is a *mens rea* issue not *actus reus*, so returning it can still be theft if, for example, he intended to permanently deprive the owner of it but changed his mind.

b) There may be no dishonesty if he shows that he believed his flat-mate would have consented in the circumstances, **s 2 (1) (b)**.

c) There may be no dishonesty if he shows he believed he had a legal right to it, **s 2 (1) (a)**.

d) There may be no dishonesty if he shows he believed the owner cannot be traced by taking reasonable steps, **s 2 (1) (c)**, but it may be hard to convince the jury as he could have reported the find to the police who could have traced the owner.

Now test yourself

7

Brief facts	Principle	Case name and section
D switched labels on goods in a supermarket.	Appropriation can be any adverse interference with property.	*Morris* **s 3**
D knew she'd been overpaid but left the money in her bank account.	If money is received under an obligation (e.g. to return it) the money still belongs to the giver.	*A-G's Reference (No 1 of 1983)* **s 5**
D took some body parts from the Royal College of Surgeons.	Body parts can be 'property' if they have been changed in some way.	*Kelly and Lindsay* **s 4**
D took the 'knowledge' from an exam paper.	Knowledge is not property.	*Oxford v Moss* **s 4**
D took some leftover scrap metal.	A person can have possession or control of property without knowing of its existence.	*Woodman* **s 4**
D was given money and a television.	Appropriation can occur even if D is given the property.	*Hinks* **s 3**
D spent the money given to her to pay bills on Christmas presents.	If there is an obligation to deal with the property in a certain way, not doing so can be theft.	*Davidge v Burnett* **s 5**
D took his own car back without paying for the repairs.	It is possible to steal your own property if someone else has possession or control.	*Turner* **s 5**
D persuaded the manager of a shop to accept two stolen cheques in return for the goods.	Appropriation can occur even if the owner consents.	*Gomez* **s 3**
D took some doors from his council flat.	D had treated the property as his own and this is enough for intent to permanently deprive.	*Lavender* **s 6**
D took an abandoned car.	D is not dishonest if he believed he had a right to take the property.	*Small* **s 2 (1) (a)**
D took a film from the cinema where he worked and copied it.	There is no intent to permanently deprive if goods are returned in the same state.	*Lloyd* **s 6**
D took money from the office safe.	Even where there is an intention to return the property it can be theft if D treated the money as his own.	*Velumyl* **s 6**

Check your understanding: 2 Application practice

2 Taking someone's basket is appropriation under **s 3** Theft Act 1968. As soon they snatched it the Ds assumed her rights to it. The bag is clearly property under **s 4** and it belongs to the person carrying it so **s 5** is also satisfied. None of the three things specified in **s 2** as not being dishonest applies here so the *Ghosh* test must be used. Wrenching the basket from a person's hand is likely to be seen as dishonest by the standards of ordinary people and it is likely that the Ds would realise this so the test is satisfied. Finally, regarding the theft, it would seem that the basket was appropriated with intent permanently to deprive the owner of it as required by **s 6**, as there is no evidence to the contrary. As force was used it may be robbery. Wrenching it from her hand shows that force has been used 'at the time' and 'in order to' steal it. It is clear from *Corcoran v Anderton* that force can be slight.

As for *mens rea*, we have already shown the *mens rea* for theft, and the *mens rea* for robbery is that the force or threat of it must be intentional or reckless. The Ds appear to have intended to use force; this can be seen in the wrenching of the bag from the person concerned. All the elements of theft are satisfied and with the added force used at the time of stealing and in order to steal the basket, the Ds can be charged with robbery.

Chapter 7

Now test yourself

1

B & S Leathley (1979)	A freezer container which had been in the same place for some time and was likely to remain there was found to be a building.
Norfolk Constabulary v Seekings and Gould (1986)	A trailer with electricity and shutters used as a temporary store was not found to be a building.
Walkington (1979)	A conviction for burglary was upheld when D went behind the counter in a shop and opened the till.
Collins (1972)	The windowsill was not 'substantial' entry and D may not have been a trespasser as he was invited in.
Brown (1985)	Leaning through a shop window to reach goods inside was effective entry. The CA said the word 'substantial' was unnecessary.
Jones and Smith (1976)	Although a boy had a right to be in his father's house this did not extend to stealing the television as he had gone beyond any permission given.

Check your understanding: 1 Application practice

1 Martin has committed burglary. He enters the bedroom as a trespasser as he has no permission to be there. As in *Walkington*, he does not have permission to be in 'part of the building', the bedroom. He knows or is certainly reckless as to the fact that he is a trespasser (*Collins*). It is most likely to be

s 9 (1) (b) because having entered any building or part of a building as a trespasser he steals, but he does not seem to have intent at the time he goes into the bedroom. Nevertheless, he has both the AR and MR of theft. However, it could be s 9 (1) (a) depending on when he formed the intent. If he formed the intent to steal before he entered the bedroom, this section is also satisfied. It does not matter that there was no intent when he entered the house, as the bedroom is 'part of a building'. If he doesn't actually take the jewellery it can still be burglary under s 9 (1) (a) if he enters the bedroom as a trespasser with intent to steal. It does not matter if he actually does so or not. It cannot be burglary under (b) as this requires that he either steals or attempts to do so.

Chapter 8

Now test yourself

1   The three parts to the *actus reus* of blackmail are:
    - a demand
    - the demand is unwarranted
    - the demand is made with menaces
2   The offence is found in **s 21** Theft Act 1968.
3   The point made in *Treacy* was that if a demand is contained in a letter the demand is made as soon as the letter is posted.
4   The demand was not found to be blackmail in *Harry* because the shopkeepers were unconcerned so there was no 'menace'.

Check your understanding: 1 Application practice

1   He could be guilty of theft which is to dishonestly appropriate property belonging to another with the intention of permanently depriving the other of it, **s 1**. Theft Act 1968. The car is property under **s 4** and it belongs to another; the person from whom he took it. Appropriation means to assume the rights of the owner (**s 3**/*Gomez*) and this is satisfied as he has assumed the right to drive the car. The (**s 2**) exceptions don't seem to apply but he would be seen as acting dishonestly in the view of ordinary people and would be aware of this, so fails the *Ghosh* test. Under **s 6** an intention permanently to deprive the owner of the car includes to treat it as his own to dispose of regardless of the other's rights. As the return of the car was subject to a demand for payment this was inconsistent with the rights of the owner to his own car. He can therefore be convicted of theft even if he returns the car.

    He may be guilty of robbery under **s 8** which is to steal, and immediately before or at the time of doing so to use force on any person or put any person in fear of force. Theft has been proved so the question is whether the use of force makes it robbery. Even a small amount of force is enough (*Clouden*) and here he used a metal bar; it would also seem this was done 'in order to' steal the car so will be robbery.

    The third possible charge is blackmail. This is where D makes an unwarranted demand with menaces. **S 21** states a demand is unwarranted unless D believed he had

reasonable grounds for making the demand; and the use of the menaces was a proper means of enforcing the demand. Even if he felt he was justified in taking the car, the means used were unlawful so unwarranted (*Harvey*). As regards 'menaces', in *Clear*, it was said that a threat which would affect a normal person would be menaces. As violence has already occurred (when the car was taken) it is likely that a normal person would be scared by the demand in these circumstances. As for *mens rea* this is that D acts with a view to gain for himself or another, or with intent to cause loss to another. He intended to gain the money he demanded for the return of the car, and also (though both are not needed) to cause the loss of the money to the owner. He may also be guilty of blackmail.

N.B. In the actual case the conviction was for robbery.

Now test yourself

5   Use the summary diagram at the end of the chapter to check your answer, then write it up on a card and keep it for revision.

Check your understanding: 2 Application practice

2   There was a demand, and even if D felt it was justified it is unlikely he thought this was a proper means of enforcing the demand so it was unwarranted, as in *Harvey*. The gun shows it was with menaces as normal people are likely to feel frightened by this which the CA said was enough in *Garwood*. Finally, there was a view to gain (the morphine) and although both are not needed, there was also an intent to cause loss to the doctor (of the morphine).

Chapter 9

Now test yourself

1   Under the *Ghosh* test there are two questions:
    - Was D's act dishonest by the ordinary standards of reasonable and honest people?
    - Did D realise the act would be regarded as dishonest by such people?
2   The representation in *Barnard* was both by conduct (wearing the cap and gown) and spoken (saying he was a member).
3   If you use a credit card, you are implying that you have authority to do so.
4   This may be fraud if you do not have the bank's authority, as in *Lambie*.

Check your understanding: 1

1   An electrician charges for rewiring a house but does not do it.
2   An unskilled worker pretends to be a qualified electrician, and so obtains payment for rewiring a house at a higher rate than for an unskilled worker.
3   An unskilled worker pretends to be a qualified electrician, intending to obtain payment for rewiring a house. This is enough even if he is not actually paid.

Now test yourself

5

Case	Brief facts	Principle
McDavitt (1981)	D refused to pay for his meal but stayed in the restaurant until the police came.	D must 'make off' so there is no offence unless and until D leaves the scene.
Troughton (1987)	D was drunk and asked a taxi driver to take him home. They had an argument and he ran off before getting home.	The service must be completed (or the goods supplied) and if not there is no offence.
Vincent (2001)	It had been agreed that payment for hotel bills could be delayed.	If payment on the spot is not expected there is no offence.
Allen (1985)	D left his hotel without paying the bill but said he intended to pay later.	D must intend not to pay permanently or there is no offence.

Check your understanding: 2 Application practice

4 In *Ray*, they could possibly be charged with all three offences. **S 2** of the Fraud Act provides that it is an offence if D dishonestly makes a false representation, intending to make a gain or cause a loss. There is an implied false representation that they would pay for the meal, and they intended to gain the price of the meal. They waited until the waiter left the room before they ran out, which could indicate dishonesty. However, it could be that they did not make the representation dishonestly, because they only decided not to pay after the meal. This would also mean that at the time of the representation it was not false. If this charge fails, the alternative under **s 11** may succeed: obtaining services dishonestly. They have obtained services (the serving of the meal) on the basis that payment will be made (they are in a restaurant) and without such payment being made (they ran out) so the *actus reus* is satisfied. As regards *mens rea*, they know the service was provided on the basis it would be paid for and again running out indicates dishonesty. The only problem with this charge is that the services must be obtained by a 'dishonest act'. When they obtained the serving of the meal they had not acted dishonestly – there was no dishonest act until they ran off without paying – so it cannot be proved that they obtained the services by this act. That leaves the final charge of making off without payment under **s 3** of the Theft Act. Here they have clearly 'made off', unlike the case of *McDavitt* where he had not left the restaurant. They know payment on the spot is expected and they have not paid for the meal or services supplied. They waited until the waiter left the room before they ran out, and this is likely to be seen as dishonest by most people and they would know this, therefore satisfying the *Ghosh* test. Finally, they intended to avoid payment permanently, as required by *Allen*. This is the charge that is most likely to succeed.

Chapter 10

Check your understanding

1 The *actus reus* is destroying or damaging property belonging to another without lawful excuse. The furniture belonged to his neighbour and he had no reason for his actions so the *actus reus* is satisfied. The *mens rea* is intent or recklessness as to the damage. This is also satisfied because he intended to set fire to the furniture. The last element of *mens rea* is intent or recklessness as to whether life is endangered by such damage. It is not necessary for life to be in danger, only for D to intend or be reckless as to this. This element is not satisfied if he knew the design would protect people, but if he did not know this then he was at least reckless as to endangering life and so would be guilty. (On the facts his conviction was upheld by the CA but this was before the HL decided that recklessness was subjective only.)

Now test yourself

1 In *Miller*, D accidentally started a fire on a mattress but then moved to another room and damage was caused by the fire.

2 The omission was failing to do anything about it.

3 He had a duty because he had created a dangerous situation, so had a duty to do something about it.

4 The offence would be arson under **s 1 (1)** and **s 1 (3)** as he did not have *mens rea* for endangering life but he had both AR and MR for the basic offence of criminal damage under **s 1 (1)** and the damage was by fire so also **s 1 (3)**.

5 He was found guilty because he had committed criminal damage and had no lawful excuse, so had AR for the basic offence under **s 1 (1)**. He may not have intended damage but he knew of the risk that the fire would cause damage which is recklessness, so he has MR. The damage was caused by fire so under **s 1 (3)** the charge is arson.

Chapter 11

Now test yourself

1 The *Graham* test is that D was compelled to act because there was good cause (or 'reasonably belief' – *Hasan*) to fear serious injury or death and a sober person of reasonable firmness, sharing the characteristics of the accused, would have responded in that way.

2 This partly depends on your chosen case but applying it to *Wadsworth*, we can say that as she had lived in fear of violence in the past she had good cause to believe the threat; it was also reasonable to believe it and in the circumstances it is likely that a sober person of reasonable firmness would have acted in a similar way.

3 Yes it can apply to family and friends and, since *Hasan*, to someone whom D feels responsible for.

4 Case examples include *Conway* where the threat was to his passenger and *Martin* where the threat was both from and to his wife.

5 In *Valderrama-Vega*, the death threat could support the defence but not the threat to disclose his homosexuality.

Check your understanding: Case example

1

Requirements of the defence of duress as stated by the HL in *Hasan*	Earlier case on the same point
The threat relied on must be to cause death or serious injury.	*Valderrama-Vega (1985)*
The criminal conduct which it is sought to excuse has been directly caused by the threats.	*Cole (1994)*

Requirements of the defence of duress as stated by the HL in *Hasan*	Earlier case on the same point
The threat must be directed to D or a member of D's family, or to 'a person for whose safety the defendant would reasonably regard himself as responsible'.	*Martin (1989)* in relation to family and *Conway (1989)* to friends. Note that *Hasan (2005)* suggests it can extend to anyone D has (or believes has) a responsibility for.
D may rely on duress only if there was no evasive action that could reasonably have been taken.	*Gill (1963)* Note that *Hudson and Taylor (1971)* was disproved in *Hasan*.
The questions for the jury were *both* objective.	*Graham (1982)* Note that it wasn't fully clear in *Graham, but the first part of the test indicates D must 'reasonably believe' there was a threat and it is now confirmed the test is objective.*
The defence is not available where, as a result of a voluntary association with criminals, D 'ought reasonably to have foreseen' the risk of violence.	*Sharp (1987)*

Chapter 12

Check your understanding: 1

1 You may have other, equally valid, arguments, but here are a couple of ideas.

For: The doctors believed the patient should be allowed to die as he had no hope of recovery. The decision was therefore in the best interests of the patient, and his family who were also suffering knowing he would not recover. The court made the right decision, although it can be said that doctors should be able to decide without going to court. Someone who believes in natural law might say that it is immoral to take a life in any circumstances, but Mill might say that the law should not interfere and the doctors and family should decide.

Against: This decision gives doctors a moral problem. Many would not want to withdraw life support because they believe that life is sacred. It is also immoral to take a life and should also be illegal whatever the circumstances. Mill might have said that the law should not interfere in individual rights, but he also said this may not apply where harm is caused to others, and the patient will die so there is clearly 'harm'.

Now test yourself

1 Three differences between law and morals are any three from the chart on page 86.

2 Hart believed law and morals to be separate.

3 Hart said that the law could be involved in a moral issue where there was a risk of harming someone.

4 A natural law follower would believe law and morals to be linked.

Check your understanding: 2

2 In *Pretty*, she was asking for a positive act by her husband (to assist her in committing suicide) to be allowed, and

the decision was that this would not be acceptable. In *Re B* she wanted treatment stopped so that she would die naturally and this was acceptable. *Bland* was on similar facts to the latter case, where the HL held that withdrawal of life support was an omission not a positive act so the doctors would not be liable for murder if they withdraw life-sustaining treatment or food.

3 *Pretty* was followed by *Purdy (2009)*, where a woman wanted the DPP to issue firmer guidance on whether her husband would be prosecuted if he helped her to die. The HL held such guidance should be clarified, but refused to rule that the husband should not be prosecuted.

Now test yourself

5 A shared morality would be one where people agreed on moral issues. Not having this is important because if there is no shared opinion on whether something is morally right, it is arguable that the law should leave matters to individual choice.

6 Intoxication is rarely allowed as a defence as it would be morally wrong for D to use being drunk as an excuse to commit a crime.

7 In *R v R* the law changed to keep up with changing social values. The court held a man could be convicted of raping his wife. Previously there was implied consent by the wife to sex within marriage.

8 In *Quintavalle v Human Fertilisation and Embryology Authority (2005)*, the law changed to keep up with medical advances by allowing for tissue-typing.

Check your understanding: 3

4 In *Brown*, it would appear that the majority of the judges decided as they did because most thought that the actions were immoral and society needed protecting against immoral behaviour. In *Wilson*, although there was also violence it was between husband and wife and a different decision was reached because this was not seen as immoral; society did not need protecting from this type of behaviour.

Chapter 13

Now test yourself

1 The theory of justice which regards law as coming from a higher source is natural law.

2 One argument in favour of the utilitarian approach to justice is that it produces an overall benefit as it seeks to maximise the greatest good for the majority of society.

3 An argument against this approach is that it ignores individual rights.

4 The theory of justice which is based on rules and ignores any moral content is positivism.

Check your understanding

1 A utilitarian would argue that to achieve the greatest benefit for the greatest number the operation should be allowed because Mary would die with or without it, whereas Jodie had a high chance of a healthy life if the operation took place.

2 This is a matter of opinion. It can be argued that the parents should be the ones to decide such a personal issue as this. On the other hand if the operation did not take place Jodie would probably have died and she deserved justice too.

3 This depends on your previous answer. As seen above a utilitarian would argue for the operation to take place but a follower of natural law is more likely to see the taking of Mary's life as immoral and therefore see the decision as unjust.

4 Again, this is a matter of opinion. If the people concerned do not agree then someone has to make a decision; arguably justice is better served by a judge deciding the issue. However, in cases such as this, one party will clearly believe that justice has not been achieved.

5 There is no 'right' answer to this. The doctors are probably in a better position to make the decision based on medical and scientific knowledge rather than emotion and/or religion. However, it is difficult to argue that parents should not be able to decide something that involves the life and death of their children. Justice for them was not achieved. On balance the right to life for Jodie overrode both the rights of the parents and the right to life for Mary, albeit a short and possibly non-existent one.

Now test yourself

5

Natural law	This theory says law comes from a higher source – nature or God – and a just law must be moral.	**Aristotle** and **Aquinas**
Positivism	This theory says law is based on clear rules and is separate from morality.	**Hart** and **Kelsen**
Utilitarianism	This theory says a just law is one which maximises happiness.	**Bentham** and **Mill**
Economic theories	These theories attempt to measure happiness in economic terms.	**Marx**, **Rawls** and **Nozick**
Substantive justice	This is whether a particular law is just.	**Hart**
Procedural justice	This is whether the legal system and institutions achieve justice.	**Hart**
Distributive justice	This is where benefits and burdens are distributed fairly through society.	**Aristotle**
Corrective justice	This is how the law can correct injustice.	**Aristotle**

Chapter 14

Now test yourself

1 A judge may need to be creative because technology and medical advances mean the law may not cover the situation.

2 Hart say judges must 'fill in the gaps' because rules are indeterminate, i.e. they have an 'open texture'.

3 Lord Denning also said this.

4 Dworkin argues that judges are merely applying existing principles and not making law.

5 The basic rule of precedent is *stare decisis* or let the decision stand.

6 The Practice Statement applies only to the Supreme Court (previously to the House of Lords).

7 Distinguishing applies to any court.

8 The CA criminal division can overrule its own earlier decisions if not doing so would cause injustice.

9 The literal rule does not allow any creativity because the judge must follow the exact words of the Act.

10 Hansard may help judges to know what Parliament's intention or purpose was because it shows the debates in Parliament during the passing of the Act.

11 The literal rule was used in *Fisher v Bell*.

12 The golden rule can be used where use of the literal rule would lead to absurdity.

Check your understanding: 1

1 a) Overruling is good because if an old law is unjust it can be changed depending on the circumstances of the case, as in *R v R* where the court protected the wife. However, it is also a bad thing because it can lead to uncertainty and, especially in the criminal law, people should know what is prohibited – *R v R* can be used to support this argument too.

   b) The literal rule is good because it means consistency in the law but can be bad because it may not give effect to Parliament's intentions, as in *Fisher v Bell*.

   c) The purposive approach is good because it takes into account Parliament's purpose in passing the Act, as in *Jones v Tower Boot Co*. However, it can be seen as bad because it is hard for judges to know what that purpose is, especially when interpreting an old Act, although they are now allowed to consult Hansard so that is an improvement.

2 One argument against judges being creative is that they are not elected and it is better for Parliament to debate fully and vote on the issue before passing a law. Another argument is that judge-made law applies retrospectively which does not seem fair to the people who have been found liable for something that was previously not against the law.

3 One argument for creativity is that the law can keep up with changing times, as in *R v R*. Another is that not being creative, as in *Fisher v Bell*, may not give effect to what Parliament was trying to achieve by passing the Act.

Check your understanding: 2 Exam practice

4 The example paragraph identifies the rules but goes no further in explaining how they are used or which rules allow creativity. It touches on which courts have to follow which rules but only barely. Overall there is nothing of substance which addresses the question of whether the rules of precedent allow judges to be creative, which is why it would not earn marks. It would not take a lot of work to earn the extra marks, however. Here is a better alternative:

The main rule of precedent is *stare decisis* which means let the decision stand. This does not allow for any creativity by judges, as they must follow earlier decisions and not be innovative. However, any judge in any court can distinguish a previous decision and so not follow it, which allows for a lot of creativity, but only where the material facts are different. A further point on this rule, which means even more flexibility and thus the opportunity for creativity, is that it is the later judge who decides which facts are material. Although this allows for creativity, different judges may decide different facts are material and so some may be creative and others not. Also a previous decision can be overruled by any higher court and the Supreme Court can use the **Practice Statement** to overrule its own decisions as it did in *Gemmell and Richards*. This case is an example of how judges can be creative and thus provide better justice. However, although the **Practice Statement** allows judges to be creative it only applies if a case gets to a higher court, and few cases go as far as the Supreme Court. This means that although some important precedents have been set and others overruled in the SC (and previously the House of Lords) these are few and far between. Another reason for this is reluctance to use the **Practice Statement** in the interests of consistency. The Court of Appeal can overrule itself in certain circumstances as set out in *Young*, but these are limited and only apply to the CA so do not allow much creativity.

This paragraph (270 words) identifies the rules and then goes further in explaining how they are used and which rules allow creativity. This would earn marks because the focus is on creativity not the rules of precedent alone. It is only an opening paragraph but highlights the main ways that precedent allows for creativity. More case illustrations and examples elaborating on these points would be needed in the body of the essay.

Chapter 15

Now test yourself

1 The fault element in criminal law is the *mens rea* of a crime.

2 The defence of intoxication is only a defence to a crime where the *mens rea* (fault) is intention. This reflects the degree of fault because if there is intent there is a high level of fault, but even where the *mens rea* is recklessness, a lower level of fault, D is deemed sufficiently at fault (by getting intoxicated) to be found reckless.

3 The HL changed the law in *Gemmell and Richards* so that recklessness is now subjective, a higher degree of fault than objective recklessness.

4 Fault may have an effect on sentencing because aggravating and mitigating factors are taken into account. These factors can indicate a greater or lesser amount of fault, or blameworthiness.

5 The fault element in the tort of negligence is that if D does not reach the standard of a reasonable person then the duty of care has been breached.

6 The rule that children are judged against a child of similar age rather than a reasonable adult recognises that children are less likely to see the risk of harm and so are not at fault to the same degree as an adult would be.

7 The breach factors affect fault in negligence because they show how much care has been taken. If D has done all that is expected of the reasonable person to avoid the risk of harm, then there is insufficient fault for liability.

8 The defence of contributory negligence reflects the degree of fault involved by allowing for damages to be reduced in accordance with the amount that C is also at fault.

Check your understanding: 1

1

Level of fault	Defence
Recognises D is not fully responsible due to an abnormality of mental functioning, so there is a reduced level of fault.	Diminished responsibility
D has lost control for a specified reason, so there is a reduced level of fault.	Loss of control
D is not at fault at all because of a total loss of control.	Automatism
D is not fully responsible so there is a reduced level of fault and a special verdict.	Insanity
This can negate the *mens rea* of intent but not recklessness, so reduces but does not remove fault.	Voluntary intoxication

Check your understanding: 2

2 **a)** The level of fault in *Stone and Dobinson* does not seem very high because they did try to take care of her, and it was not only their fault that she died. It was mainly because she refused to eat. In gross negligence manslaughter cases the fault element is low and it is arguable that the *mens rea* should be at least subjective recklessness for all crimes, especially serious ones. One point is that their attempt at taking care would be seen as a mitigating factor so could be taken into account when sentencing.

b) Although in *Nedrick*, D had *mens rea* for the act of setting the fire (arson) he did not have any *mens rea* for the death. Unlawful act manslaughter has a very low level of fault as *mens rea* is only needed as regards the unlawful act. This seems too low a level of fault for a serious crime.

c) In *Nettleship v Weston*, it is arguable that a learner has a lower level of fault than a competent driver who would be better able to handle the car. She should perhaps be judged against another learner in the same way that a child is judged against another child of the same age (as in *Mullins v Richard*). This would reflect her inexperience and lack of any high level of fault.

Chapter 16

Now test yourself

1 The interests of the parents (whose religious beliefs were that life was sacrosanct), the hospital (who wanted to save a life) and those of the child (who would be able to have a life) were in conflict in *Re A*. Also, public interests conflicted as some groups believed it was wrong to take a life even to save another, whereas others believed it was best to give one child the chance of a full and healthy life.

2 The court balanced the interests by looking at who would gain the most benefit and ruling that the operation should go ahead.

3 The dominant theory of justice was a utilitarian one, because the decision reflected the idea that the most interests would be satisfied if the operation was performed.

4 Pound means that law can be used to engineer a balance between conflicting interests in order to regulate society and build the best structure possible.

5 A utilitarian would engineer the balance between conflicting interests so that the maximum benefit for the most people was achieved.

6 The dominant interest in cases involving intoxication is the public interest.

7 There are many examples and you may have chosen different ones, but here is one from each area:

- An example from the substantive law is *Hill v CC of West Yorkshire*, where the interests of the victim (and her mother) were in conflict with the public interest. The police did not owe a duty because it was not in the public interest and could make policing less effective.

- An example from the legal process is the right of D to bail and the interests of the public in being safe. When balancing these interests the court will normally favour D and grant bail, but if the crime is murder the balance tips in favour of protecting the public interest, so bail is usually refused.

Check your understanding: 1

1 The interests in conflict in *Miller v Jackson* were the victim's private interest and the wider public interest.

2 They conflicted because she wanted the quiet enjoyment of her garden but the public interest was in having sporting and social activities.

3 The conflict was resolved by the court awarding her damages as compensation but not awarding an injunction to stop the cricket.

4 Justice was probably achieved according to utilitarianism because more people gained a benefit.

5 This is a matter of opinion. People who do not enjoy sports would probably say not, but cricket fans would say justice was done, and so would many others who may not be 'sporty' but who regard sporting activities as beneficial to the community.

Check your understanding: 2

6

The interest	The conflict	The success of the law
Freedom of expression	There is often a conflict between individual rights or freedoms as one person's freedom may interfere with another's, as in freedom of speech and the right not to be defamed. There is also the public interest in keeping state secrets which will be in conflict with those who believe in openness.	The law has been quite successful in the attempt to balance private interests by incorporating the **European Convention on Human Rights** but also having laws against defamation. The law in relation to the private vs. the public interest has been less successful as many believe that governments need to be more open with the public, but the law has protected the public interest in various cases where an individual has leaked information.
Donoghue v Stevenson and the Consumer Protection Act 1987	The interests of a consumer not to be harmed conflict with those of a manufacturer not to be sued where there is no contract. The public interest would be in having consumers in general protected from negligent manufacturers.	The law has been successful here because a duty of care was established in *Donoghue* which protected not only that individual consumer but also the public as a whole. The manufacturer also had some protection because there is no liability if care is taken. The CPA goes further as now a manufacturer is strictly liable so there is no need to prove negligence. This protects the public but is arguably unfair on manufacturers. However, a manufacturer is more able to insure against this so overall the balance is fair.
The mandatory sentence for murder	The interests of the individual offender to be sentenced according to the level of fault involved, against the private interests of victims of violent crime and also the public interests of society to be safe from violence.	The law has not really been successful here because judges are prevented from being fair to individual offenders by considering any mitigating circumstances. The public interest prevails at the expense of the individual, supporting Pound's view that public and private interests should not be balanced against each other.
Anti-terrorism laws which allow people to be detained without charge	The interests of the individual in freedom of movement are in conflict with those of the public and the state to be safe from harm.	Laws dealing with the threat of terrorism have been controversial and some argue that here the law has not been effective in achieving a just balance as individual rights are subordinated to the interests of state security. Innocent people can be locked up without a trial, and this is not what most would regard as justice. It can be argued that when state security is an issue the law cannot achieve an effective balance as the public interest will always prevail.